WRITING THE SELF-ELEGY

WRITING THE SELF-ELEGY

The Past Is Not Disappearing Ink

Edited by Kara Dorris

Southern Illinois University Press
Carbondale

Southern Illinois University Press
www.siupress.com

26 25 24 23   4 3 2 1

Cover illustration: Woman holding mirror.
Shutterstock photo 2048751800 by Cristina Conti.

Library of Congress Cataloging-in-Publication Data
Names: Dorris, Kara Delene, 1980– editor.
Title: Writing the self-elegy : the past is not disappearing ink / edited
by Kara Dorris.
Description: Carbondale : Southern Illinois University Press, [2023] |
Summary: "Self-elegies are cultural artifacts, lenses for understanding
and defining self as well as sharing and creating community.The po-
ems and prose in this anthology are a mix of autobiography and poet-
ics, incorporating craft with race, gender, sexuality, ability/disability,
and place"—Provided by publisher.
Identifiers: LCCN 2022046526 (print) | LCCN 2022046527 (ebook) |
ISBN 9780809339068 (paperback) | ISBN 9780809339075 (ebook)
Subjects: LCSH: Self-Literary collections. | American literature—
21st century. | Poetics. | LCGFT: Autobiographical poetry. | Essays.
Classification: LCC PS509.S375 2023 (print) |
LCC PS509.S375 2023 (ebook) |
DDC 808.8/0384--dc23/eng/20230124
LC record available at https://lccn.loc.gov/2022046526
LC ebook record available at https://lccn.loc.gov/2022046527

Printed on recycled paper ♻

SIU
Southern Illinois University System

For anyone who has ever gazed
into the past and wondered *what if*

I'm looking for the face I had, before the world was made
— W.B. Yeats

One lives in the hope of becoming a memory
— Antonio Porchia

open me carefully
— Emily Dickinson

CONTENTS

WRITING THE SELF-ELEGY

Handmade Ink

An Introduction

"someone will remember us // I say // even in another time"
— Sappho, fragment 147 (Anne Carson, trans.)

For as long as I can remember, I have been inclined towards the writerly life, towards observation and introspection. Eventually, this tendency manifested itself as poetry, then as self-elegy. Although I began coordinating this anthology long before the pandemic, the forced isolation and social distancing lends itself to self-interrogation and retrospection. Who hasn't reached back into time, found a moment that felt unfinished, a moment we wished had ended different, a moment that still haunts and defines us? Who doesn't wonder, *what if*?

When I was fifteen, I failed my typing class. Horribly. I had little mobility in my left wrist, my dominant wrist. No matter how I sat and adjusted my body, I could barely twist my wrist so that the palm faced downward into the correct typist's position. I would hold my elbow, out high, sometimes as high as my shoulder, as if always on the verge of asking permission to find that palm-down range, but still the arm that is three inches shorter than it should be does not make a very effective typing tool. To increase my mobility, doctors took out the radial bone in my forearm, turned it over like a question in an experiment, and then screwed it upside down back into my arm. They succeeded, I guess, because now I can type fast and turn my palm downward fairly easily. Of course, don't ask me to cup loose change in my left hand because now turning my palm upwards forces a strange contortion of twisting my elbow into my ribs, a kind of reverse arabesque. Through these experiences and others, my genetic bone disorder has shaped my identity. If I could travel back in time, what could I offer that girl on the surgical table? Who could I have been without these metal plates? These questions began my path towards self-discovery through poetry and, eventually, the self-elegy, a kind of poetry that mourns aspects of the self that are lost, abandoned, or maybe never existed at all.

For me, one of those lost selves could have been a professional dancer. I have always loved ballet, tap, jazz; as a teenager I even tried pointe once, braced with ankle braces and sheer will, unwilling to believe I could not make my body conform to song and imagination. The dancer believes in her body, in its beauty, muscle memory, teachableness. She knows, but refuses to believe, that the body is temporary; instead, it becomes mythological, beyond natural explanation. Each dance is a suspended moment when decline is briefly forgotten, a space where the dancer can narrate herself into being, like a speaker in a poem. The dancer must believe in her body's reliability and believe that her passion, her will is enough.

Even as we believe the body is reliable, it is not; even as we believe passion is enough, sometimes it is not. I see these suspended beliefs and disbeliefs in poetry, in the struggle and failure to translate experience into words, and I have always wondered how this knowledge and the resistance to it can coexist. I am suspended by the secret hope, my mother's hope, that *I can be anything I want to be*—although, ultimately, I fail more than I succeed. Still, there is a version of myself I keep in my mind: I am twenty pounds lighter, graceful and poised, and I can quote Rilke and other poetry greats from memory. There are versions of myself that I pour into my poems: the daughter of a depressive and homeless meth user, the sister to a cancer survivor. There are versions I present to my students: confident, experienced, educated poet. There are versions no one sees when I am nothing, Celan's *No-One's-Rose*. I guess the truth lies somewhere in between. Can I mourn the versions I never knew? The versions I have left behind? What consolation can I achieve?

And this brings me to the self-elegy. Reading elegy after elegy—including but not limited to Emily Dickinson's "I died for beauty but was scarce," Sylvia Plath's "Lady Lazarus," Brenda Shaughnessy's "Advice to My Twenty-Four-Year-Old Self"—I have been struck by the moments in which poets mourned aspects of *themselves* as well as others.

Today, in a time when "selfies" are popular, even leading to the invention of the "selfie stick," it is not surprising that we would become more internally reflective while externally revealing our most personal desires. Historically, we have been trying to understand and share ourselves long before the invention of smart phones and filters—Narcissus staring at himself in water, bronze and silver-backed mirrors, artistic self-portraits by Rembrandt, Van Gogh, Kahlo, Sherman. Even the first recorded selfie, a daguerreotype taken in 1839, acts as a memorial and decorates its subject's tombstone. Today, you can step into 3D selfie machines, recreating and preserving an exact moment. An image is rarely just an image but a way of seeing, a reminder, a collection of choices and feelings that blend to create a singular experience. As long as we fear being forgotten, fear losing what we love, fear death, we will try to preserve, catalog, and share our lives. Familiar or not, this fear feels no less relevant.

Social media has made cataloging and sharing our lives even easier. When we add in the forced isolation of a global pandemic, hindsight, and what if possibilities, the fear of missing out becomes even more urgent. I wonder, if we wrote notes for our pandemic selves, what would we say? Who were we before? Who will be after? That's where the self-elegy comes in. To catalogue the good and bad, known and unknown, what could be or might never be.

For me, the self-elegy is reflective, reinventive, and confrontational, interrogating and elegizing past versions of self. To say self-elegy is new would be naive; as I read numerous elegies, from Shakespeare's Sonnet 71 to Laura Kasischke's "Space, in Chains," I found moments of self-elegizing—for how can we truly mourn another without mourning the self that was created through that relationship? Yet, this awareness of self (and how the self is created) seems more prevalent than ever before. With self in the description, when the self is often considered an individualized construct, does a self-elegy have to *only* mourn the self or an aspect of the self to be classified as a self-elegy? And if so, why would we want to impose such a limitation?

Sometimes I think comparing contemporary self-elegies to selfies is a brilliant strategy; other times, an oversimplification or even wishful thinking—both are cultural artifacts stemming from a time of accessibility, excess, and reflection; both serve as remembrances allowing us to revisit past moments; both have the potential to promote agency, urging us to control and share our own narratives even as these same mediums shape those narratives and perceptions.

At its core, isn't a selfie an artifact, a memorial of a moment gone too fast, a moment to remember, to celebrate, and ultimately mourn? Proof of a self already changing? A want? A wish? Then again, perhaps I am looking only as a poet looks at the world and sees an opportunity to stage, to reflect, to understand. Which leads us to primary motivations behind selfies and, arguably, behind self-elegies as well: defining and framing our own self-creation myths. The question is, are selfies isolationist narcissism or building blocks for self and community? Are we trying to present a false, superficial perfection, consciously or not, or are we genuinely trying to share our truest selves, warts and all? One prevents connection, the other welcomes it. And does it have to be one or the other? Let's look at my story.

Can you remember your first time? My first selfie, that I remember consciously setting out to take, was standing before the Rosetta Stone at the British Museum. It's 2001, and I'm twenty years old, wearing jeans, Diesel shoes, and an orange tank top. My long reddish-brown hair is pulled up in a messy bun. The camera is held tight against my face, my reflection reflected in glass, superimposed over stone. I wanted proof that I existed in that particular space and time. In the picture, I am more prominent than the stone, but the stone as a translation miracle informed my need to mark the moment. Without the stone, I wouldn't have stopped to take the picture. Without the glass case, my image wouldn't even have been captured, which, I guess was the point: without knowing it, I was already framing my body to hide my disability. Seven years later, I wrote my first self-elegy, "Osteochondroma Lineage," even if I didn't know it at the time, which traced the influence my hereditary bone disorder has had on my life as a way of seeing, of understanding. By writing this poem, I was better able to understand how my bone disorder frames my experiences, past and present.

Self-elegies can allow poets to question without expectation of clear answers, to analyze the self bluntly, without a coat of sugar, to be angry and melancholic at the inevitable loss time offers us. The past has a finality of death— we cannot change it, only try to understand how it influences today and tomorrow. My identity as a mourner, *as one who was born to lose everything*— emotionally and physically—defines me. Self-elegy allows me to define myself, create my own rehearsal space where I can dance between loss and self-reinvention—and hopefully, afterwards, I will better understand the world and my place in it. I will understand that disability is not shameful and does not make us less. I am not a dancer, but the dream of being one still defines me, as does the story about a failed typing class, as well as the retelling of that story in these pages. So, yes, I mourn versions of myself that never existed and versions that were left behind. I mourn that wannabe dancer who never knew genetics outweigh determination. Why not just bury those dead versions of myself? I need those versions like I need my left radial bone or intestines. It's all integral. All vital. Physical and mental skeleton and viscera. If I wrote a self-elegy to my fifteen-year-old self I would say *the self is multiple and contradictory, a fickle mystery we continuously try to unravel. So what if you hold your left elbow out like an arabesque when you type? You won't know it is wrong until someone tells you. You will lose something that day. Don't waste every day after chasing it.* Of course, she probably wouldn't have listened, but I'm listening now.

The Framing Effect

Self-elegy is self-reflection but also performance, and as performance it acts as a medium to connect to others, to share doubts, fears, and triumphs. The self-elegy can be a way to gain agency, to frame experience and knowledge, to gain understanding of self, but also to choose how that self is presented to others.

In self-elegy, *if-then* games are abound, trying to answer the question: who would I be if I had made a different choice? When investigating the past, we often vacillate between self-awareness and self-denial, trying to manage failure and acceptance, what is and what could have been. We often romanticize, we are often overly critical; this process is not all or nothing but a spectrum, and the self-elegy can be a useful navigational tool. Although we can't always choose what happens to us, we can choose the way we see it—even if self-elegy can never offer a completely objective or comprehensive view. And, really, what can? The poets included in this section use the stages and props available to them to frame and to define their own terms.

Singularity

In my end is my beginning.—T. S. Eliot

New Year's Eve
played out like a star

that collapses beyond a certain point
when a black hole is formed,

and inside the black hole
a singularity, all matter binding,

moving from finite to infinite,
a new thing born—

while the rest of the world was out
at parties, I was at home,

neither celebrating
nor lamenting, alone,

except for the two million people
in my living room,

watching the giant silver orb
descend and delete time,

the ball like a star
about to explode, go supernova,

and at the precise moment
the year turned over, the word *alone*—

an event horizon around a black hole
that marks the point of no return—

amassed then buckled,
the way a body falls inward

when crushed by its own gravity,
and a new singularity

emerged—*alone*—only now
on the other side of the new year

with people on TV cheering,
kissing, as if stellar remnants

had blasted off to Times Square
and the crowd was a nebula, an anomaly,

particles in space colliding,
bright as their neon sunglasses

that blinked the date
and let me know it was time.

This is the kind of moment
when a person decides

she must go somewhere
where heartbreak is not static

and the word *alone*
does not translate

or cross oceans, fields,
but rather, is absorbed

into the dark sky
like a void left by a star

light-years away
from a crowded square at midnight,

making just enough room
to stand alone and be in it.

The Heart Has the Capacity to Break
and Reset a Million Times

But it's the million and first, say,
that begins in a cab to Woodside, Queens,

with a hockey player, who's also a musician
and a city planner, who might be a one-night stand,

but he's the best kisser you've come across
in years, with a face that's all elegy and nostalgia,

edges but smooth, the Mekong Delta in June,
the mouth, clementines flown in from another country,

what only stays on the shelves briefly before
it disappears for a year, and before you know it,

everything in you is moving in his direction,
your head gravitates to his chest, his fingers,

anywhere you can hear a stress or a pulse,
until the 4/4 beat becomes 6/8,

a compound time signature,
because he's every place you've ever

climbed or crawled that knocked the wind out,
like the Grand Canyon or the Củ Chi tunnels,

a vapor that expands to fill even the largest
of rooms, and you can't breathe, in this cab,

going to his apartment, you're 18 again
in some kid's parents' basement listening to Dylan

for the first time, stoned, or maybe not stoned,
it's that lead singer voice whispering in your ear

across 42nd Street and through the Midtown Tunnel,
and now you're 16 riding in the back of a Senior's car,

making out but not the way you did at 16;
he could be taking you anywhere, but he's taking you

back to a time before you ever fell in love,
before any transmutations of the heart,

resetting its counter, and he makes up
for every football player who ever left any girl

sitting at a table at the Junior prom to dance
with the head cheerleader, because tonight,

you are 14 and you've carried his hockey stick
through the streets of New York, the way at 14

you carried the quarterback's cleats to the bus,
and even though in the morning he'll take you

to the platform to get the train back to the city,
even though you'll both become 40 again

by the time the train rolls into the station,
even though he'll say *this but no further*

just as you turn to board, tonight, in this cab,
you are 13, your bodies unbearably strung,

lips unendurably ready, and when he leans in,
everything else in the world is forced to evacuate,

when he leans in, you are both young and beautiful
without even a trace of sadness.

Chaos Theory

If there were a haunting place,
          a space behind the eye sockets

or an inch of brain reserved
          for alternate endings,

there would be a version
          where a girl in her early twenties

will sit alone in a darkened square,
          abandoned by the boy

she is traveling with,
          who will take the money,

passports, and key to the hostel,
          and leave her

with just one cigarette,
          which she will roll

between her thumb
          and forefinger, then scissor,

this one innocuous thing
          she can control

as the men begin to hover,
          not in circles exactly,

but the random organization
          that exists in nature—

ant colony algorithms,
          particle swarm,

and then triangulation,
      the principles of flocking birds:

separation, alignment, cohesion,
      where each man

will keep an even distance
      from the other

to maintain the shape
      that is a form,

then not,
      but will become

a tight V again
      the moment she looks away.

In this version,
      instead of the boy returning

to prove his twisted point,
      that she would not survive

without him,
      the girl will remain fixed,

the point attractor
      in chaos theory,

her throat hot and dry
      as if lined by fine dust,

and the men
      will keep positioning,

veering, like birds do
      against even the most difficult wind,

a powerful force
  of collective motion,

an entity, which,
  by its very nature,

must and will
  constantly find

its own order
  and destination.

Into the Now: Time in Self-Elegy

Marvin Bell said: "What they say 'there are no words for'—that's what poetry is for." Though I have written celebratory poems and love poems, I have especially turned to poetry to make sense where sense is elusive, during those times of loss where one feels simultaneously paralyzed and ready to explode. What it means to be alone, lost relationships, or relationships that erode the self or make one question the self—these are the circumstances that evoke a longing for a way to go back in time and start again.

There's something about self-elegy that feels both nostalgic and futuristic—it's as if the poem lives in an in-between space where time collapses into the now, but where other timelines exist, whether within the poem or just outside its margins, as T. S. Eliot describes in "Burnt Norton":

Time past and time future
What might have been and what has been
Point to one end, which is always present.

Eliot also notes that "What might have been is an abstraction." Still, the self-elegy pursues what might have been, wants to explore it, to memorialize or lament it, perhaps even transform it into something more palatable as a path to consolation. For these types of poems, I think of Gaston Bachelard's *The Poetics of Space*, where he talks about how creatures in shells, like mollusks, that may appear to be stationary or to display very little motion actually have energy amassing inside their containers, a force that, in its own time, will explode.

I think of self-elegy as the place where that force is gathering, collecting—by looking backward and forward, the poem situates itself between worlds, worlds that are neither true nor false, where time folds into itself to create a new, if not better, then more informed, reality. But there's also something paradoxical about the collapse of time where multiple versions of the self exist. It's as if the self-elegy is the poetic interpretation of Schrödinger's cat, where quantum objects can exist in multiple states at once, the superposition, until they are measured or observed.

In the case of Schrödinger's cat, a theoretical cat is in a box with a sealed flask of poison that has a fifty-fifty chance of being released, such that the cat will have an equal possibility of being alive or dead upon the opening of the box. While the box is closed, the cat (not being observed) is said to be both dead and alive simultaneously in order for it to be in all its possible states. When the box is opened, superposition collapses, and only then is the cat either dead or alive. In self-elegy, the poem is like the closed box, a place where the self can exist in the superposition of multiple states, versions, or timelines. As the poem progresses, works through its truths, and analyzes and probes the loss, the box opens, and the self is rendered in a new, possibly more enlightened state.

In Franz Wright's poem "Progress," the speaker, in a profound state of aloneness in a room "with all the world's beauty and cruelty," also senses the flux of time: "What is time? When is the present?" Aloneness becomes an agent of or catalyst for its own solution. Even when the solution or the sense-making is still elusive or seemingly far off, the poem, by its act of naming and examining, seems to reduce the distance. The poem ends:

> And everything that once was
> infinitely far
> and unsayable is now
> unsayable
> and right here in the room.

That's what writing the self-elegy feels like for me—a way to bring the un-sayable just a little closer, a way to expose, investigate, and thereby defuse the loss. It's as if the poem begins from the vantage point of Schrödinger's cat or Bachelard's mollusk, which "by staying in the motionlessness of its shell . . . is preparing temporal explosions, not to say whirlwinds, of being." Within the confines and safety of this shell, all hell can break loose—wailing and head banging and fist pounding—all imperceptible to the outside world. Timelines can intersect; lost selves can be found or reimagined. Hopefully if things gestate enough and are worked through enough and refined enough, out of the opening will come the poem—revealing a new version of the self connected to both the internal chaos and external world, if not wiser then more aware, carrying a shell that simultaneously contains and releases.

Try It Yourself(ie)-Elegy: Now/Then Poem

Part 1: Then. Freewrite for fifteen minutes about a personal difficulty from your past (a loss, a disappointment, the end of a relationship, etc.). Write from the "then" perspective—the core of the experience, as if you are inside it, inhabiting the self you were then and tell the story from that perspective. Who are you? How old are you? What are you going through? What's happening in the world around you (historical facts or other markers to pin the time period)? What sensations do you feel in your body (examine all senses)? Take a 360-degree look at a physical space from this time (a room, an outdoor space, etc.)—what do you see? What's the smallest detail from this time period you can remember? What are three things you believe will happen in the future because of this situation?

Part 2: Now. Using details from part 1, write a poem from the "now" perspective, retelling the story from today's vantage point. Tell the story *about* the person who went through the difficulty, from the outside, as though you are telling someone in your present a story about someone from your past. Pick the hardest thing to explain, and describe it by comparing it to something else, some tangible thing outside of or unrelated to the story. Infuse the explanation with the language of a topic that interests you—wildlife, astronomy, the ocean, math, music, landscape, and so on. Mix this language with details from part 1 as you craft the poem. Try for layers, textures, and interesting juxtapositions. Let what you know now merge with what happened then and see if a new perspective emerges.

Girl Candela

How to be bold as a spirit? Not ruled
By bordering eye, polyphias of projection.

There are advantages to invisibility. The Elders say:
Living is more about how you manage your life.

Still, I envy the gone and sainted, so free-speaking,
So daring in immortality, ancestral fount.

How many flores grow in the teeth of the living?
They asked me to speak at a girl's funeral.

I did, for her honor, but couldn't edit my explanations;
I failed to capture her. She looked too much like me.

Running wasn't right either, so I sang insufficient hymn.
At the lip of grave: her voice turned mirror, the mirror to ghost.

That ghost turned to spirit, and the spirit, prayer.
Here are the glories of being loud without yelling, to incant

without a mourning mouth. To call for help
and see the sources of all normal Saints, candela-bright.

Here is a dream that you too, unfinished,
                                    (even today)

could feel as innocent

                                        as a completed life.

After Psalm 23

So what, pray/tell, do you want?
      After pastures don't green better?
      After the shaggiest wool is shorn?
I told you plenty of times, before you wept
yourself to heart-slaughter:

Water the forb first. Chill out.
      Don't waste time thinking about blood or meat.
No need to shiver, bone-shown, to strangers. Let shepherds lead.
        You're not an overflowing cup, but a fleshy you.
                          Lay down on your mat, at times, tire.
I'm trying to help you, little self, while you resist
      me, mid-tremble.
Dead in the valley of the shadow of death
      You are not who you have always been—
Good. Reborn wild in still waters; kid, you're fine.
      Surely, mercy is a goodness, surely mercy is your right.

Baggage

On the new lawn,
rhododendron petals
wilt in a blue
jay's mouth.

A sign, I think. Some kind of glory?

I get closer: No petals.
The jay just caught toilet paper
in her beak.

There she goes:
just dragging that shit along.

I wonder how many
flowers I think live in my teeth,
when they're just dead nothings
I carry around.

(But they're mine!)

Kinds of Grace

Beach-bidden, I see
bulges of sand and conch chunk,

banked coral, halved shells, hard
like fingernail face. Bounce of Wellcraft,

air-sprint of searching pelican.
Prasine wave, pleat of ocean ripple,

loose unbind of fulling tide.
A break of wave, another break.

Today, special and ordinary, a crowd
has formed under blazing blue.

Baby shark lies ashore, twitching.
A family reeled her in after fishing, thought

she was a large cobia, not a small blacktip.
Throw it back! Some say, others say, *eat*!

While the crowd debates, a tide rolls in,
cradles the baby's body. Like grace,

the sea carries her back home.

Projecting as Connection

After reading Kara Dorris's beautiful work on the self-elegy, I see the form as a celebratory mourning—of the cyclical deaths of the self, of those who have passed, of the many versions of ourselves living within our loved ones. While I was working on these poems, I thought about how I interpret these little cyclical deaths of the self—how do I know when I'm passing from one stage to another? What or who is dying within me? What has been reborn? Who sees these new stages of the self?

I realized so much of my understanding of the world is rooted in projection and my interpretation of these projections. I used to think of "projecting" as a negative concept, as attributing nonrealities onto things, texts, or people I know nothing about. I've come to see projecting as a form of connection. I see myself in others or feel something someone else has felt and thus learn something new about myself. Thus, that process of searching for kinship, however flawed, can lead me beyond a static sense of identity. Rather, I see myself in a dynamic, moving, interesting, passing world. When looking for myself within, I am also looking outside of myself. I'm marking who I've known, where I've gone, what I aspire to be.

I thought about how my journey is reflected in family, friends, in relationships, in animals, books, and the environment; how I see the vast and lonely gulf between me and those I know, and those who have passed on; how I can feel the incredible crackle and flame of our kinship.

These poems, then, are snapshots within snapshots of many deaths of the self, as seen through a mirrored world. They are also celebratory mournings of the many selves the speaker knows and inhabits.

Try It Yourself(ie): Another Realm

Write about your relationship to an animal. How does this animal affect how you see the world? Or write about passing through another realm. What does this passage feel like? Who or what do you find on the other side? Who might you be on the other side? Turn this into a poem.

Lives of the Artists: An Aria

Against the coldness of Autumn, the day will come on
like a chime. She'll move away & what'll settle in her shadow's

corner will be loneliness. The city will play its misdemeanors,
& its organization of loss, a contagion.

I'll pray for light, that when I die the humiliating hour will be
a handsome eyelid. I'll enter its waiting view

weary, & prayers will burn in the middle
of my tongue. I'll look into the ellipsis of memory, but I will not find
   a thing

there. I'll shake the orb of eyesight loose, & spill the ink
into a box rife with leaves, & veins, & souvenirs.   .

What will I call this transition, but *fitting*?
The sounding lines will tire. The barricade will fall.

And, this, *where space ends*, I imagine
I'll call it *death or infinity*. Spring will arrive in nothingness,

& I'll sing in my prison of reason. I'll name
the cold rain, its collectivity, I'll revisit the psalms, & upon

the water I'll praise silence. *Of the noon-day brightness*,
I'll wade into the frailty of eternity, drawing a sharp breath, & blossom.

St. George: A Lecturer's Lament

It's early morning & dawn is drunk and
at it once more, her vase of fuchsias & wood lilies

strewn oblong across the butte. I interrupt my lecture:
the *affective fallacy* & *intentional fallacy* . . .

yet nowhere can we discern what the light intends,
the emotion it draws, my students

on their tip toes, educable ballerinas
at this early hour. Sleep-laden, at 7am, they sag into

the metal of their desks, Dali-like,
& from the clearing of their consciousness

dredge the silted ground to excavate a comment.
I ask about symbolism & metaphor

in *A Raisin in the Sun*, & what I gift them later
makes them feel uncomfortable, comments on "race

restrictive covenants" and Lindner's
"Improvement Association" aren't familiar terms,

& what they gift *me* makes me feel secluded
on this southern Utah stage, the silence welling up

in both our sensibilities, delicate walls to stay the water
before the storm recedes. But I don't care

for silence, indifference's brutish step-brother,
I care for resistance to *marginalization*,

for thought to get combed back in, follicles
to breathe, the rats and ruin to decenter us dear

listeners, for the world made of exploitation
& my students awareness of it

to tremor at this our hour of the desert's bloom-driven
sun & Hansberry's uneasy depiction.

Letters to Yesteryear

1. *Nepenthe*

My father & grandfather hold silence, a blessing of winter, in their hands
God's presence, like a *Composition in the Form of a Pear*, others accuse of
    formlessness
In the in media res of day, the mind unravels there, always there
Dear delusion, how I've spent with you these eight years
November, then the white carriage of January, the humidity of August
Lonely & dying are the Aspen leaves in late fall
Morning, I wade into your river of halfmiracles & drown

2. *Testimonio*

Always the gesture that speaks
Always the speech delivered to the deafest ear
Always the ear, & the guilt that lies at the base of the drum
Always the dark light of regret—directionless
Always liquor & indifference afterward
Always the theater, the elegy for every one of us actors

3. *Narrative*

I'm told I was handsome when I was a boy
Sturdy as a tree, roots deep in the earth like rain
The world around me broke to pieces
People's voices were made of straw & the loon labored in the dusk
Memory—a dream where the sun never quite radiated
I breathed in the bird's flight & its flight took the shape of a soft vowel
Always, *vowels*, & how the *verbs* failed to form

4. *Mythology*

I look on, like some failed god, crowdweary
I drink holy water that I might not ever ingest original sin
I look for my Father in his garden of dementia
Today dies that tomorrow may live
I commit my Mother's voice to memory & to the marrow of my bones
I dream of riverbanks & how to wade into their rushing

At Daylight: A Tale w/ Half-Dead Forest

–after Ken Gonzales-Day's Searching
for California Hang Trees

Beyond the hang tree's July horizon, endless inflections
of men's voices and dogs' barking ring

at the forest's edge. I open the first door of an imagined death,
& my grandfather, a man thick

as a moss-covered trunk, his limbs scarred as fields,
greets me in the waving grass. To find

the sky, with its grey banners of morning breeze & light
as endless sleep, he points a bark-hard

finger & fixes an eye to it. This, I imagine is where
I must end my going, before the second

door of death opens. In its threshold every moment is
past, past, past, & as the midday drips through the weathered leaves,

the door greets afternoon's silence.
To stretch forth into, to hang from, forward into light,

yet having *been*, one realizes life is within
oneself, that upon death it fractals out slowly in somber colors.

Though I grow sleepy my imagined death returns,
& I can hear my grandmother's voice, caution in her tone,

the tale of the ridge,
of men leaving yet never to return until dusk, when

the dark glides into nothingness, & a horse
leads its townspeople to the tree. The riverbed quivers.

The notes of hate in the men return,
& my body is a matterless thing swinging

above their dogs sunning their bellies.
I know what I know of life is minute. It spins by

like the steely voice of God,
shaken to dust, my limbs incomprehensible now

that the third door of death has opened,
& I am left at this one's threshold,

my blood warm as July rain, earthless now,
no reason for such things to exist anymore than to wash me

free of memory, sight & sound, body & mind.
Each moment hereafter an elegy shared

for a man in disrepair, not the man himself, but his *being*
defined by the distance between heaven and hell.

Hanging on the Wall of Existence

My Poetics 1: a form of elegy, always.
My Poetics 2: an exploration of a country hell-bent on erasing Latinx identities.
My Poetics 3: a study of parts of myself that never existed.
My Poetics 4: an act of recovery.

Elegy, as I understand it, allows one to mourn, for a collective to mourn.

1.1
Being a light-skinned Latinx male living in a world eager to accept me as white yet hell-bent on erasing me is devastating; thus, writing in modes of self-elegy is very natural for me. Often, I find that I view the world in elegiac ways.

1.2
I mourn for the fact that my parents were physically abused by their teachers for speaking their native tongue, Spanish. I mourn for the fact that they were reticent to hand down this abuse to their sons. I mourn for the fact that I am not bilingual. I mourn that my mother tongue was taken from me by force. I mourn that I only speak and write in a language not my own.

1.3
Becoming, to my mind, is always a process of individuation.

1.4
From the time I was seven years old, I grew up with only one grandparent, my mother's father. I never met my mother's mother. She died when my mother was fourteen years old.

1.5

I fear that my memories are mere microfictions or mythologies. This *fear* and this kind of *loss* is part of my *becoming*.

2.1

Concerned about the world around me, I watch the TV and feel shocked that children have been stripped from their parents and are living in cages, the result of an unjust political administration. I wonder if I hadn't been born in the United States in 1973, yet was one of those kids born recently and with less fortune, if I'd ever see my parents again. I wonder if I'd learn a different language and live in a world filtered through that language. I wonder if I'd feel all such loss in a language spoken by my aggressor/country, and its unjust leader.

2.2

When my family left Europe and settled, via Mexico City, in what is now New Mexico, they weren't rapists or drug dealers. They were farmers and ranchers. The values they handed down are to protect those most vulnerable among us.

2.3

The loss my family experienced, researchers argue, remains in my DNA.

2.4

Recently I learned that I am 47.9 percent European (Spanish and Portuguese), 36 percent East Asian and Native American, 1.1 percent Ashkenazi Jewish, 9 percent Unassigned. I am in part an embodiment of the American Southwest.

2.5

As I write this, I am aware that my Latinx brothers and sisters are suffering. Some, their kids are traumatized.

3.1

When I was child, in deep distress due to domestic turmoil, I imagined that a community of Native Americans would adopt me and take me away to a better place. Perhaps this was the product of my paternal grandmother's kindness. Though I was huero, she accepted me nevertheless.

3.2

Growing up, I always wanted to look more Latinx, be accepted as Latinx, be celebrated for my Latinx background.

3.3

It wasn't until I was in my early twenties that I read a book by a Latinx member of my community. It wasn't until my early twenties that I read positive depictions of my community. It wasn't until my early twenties that I was able to celebrate my sense of self in literature. It wasn't until my early twenties that I felt seen and heard. It wasn't until my early twenties that I felt a need to contribute to my community's celebration of our selves.

3.4

I resist allowing others to define me.

3.5

What life I will image, as my very own unfolds, I will strive toward with compassion for others, with love for those who subject me to judgement, and with grace for those who impact the trajectory of who I *become*.

4.1

Recovering the past, with my community always in mind, is an act of love.

4.2

I write because I feel a sense of responsibility to do so. I write because I physically have to do so, because I have to rid the sickness of the world from my inner self so that I may live a bit more peacefully.

4.3

My first manuscript explored my own personal past, my Latinx identity, my family's history.

4.4

My first published book explored the human condition, as depicted in personae poems, wherein a sense of loss takes place among "shifting city-grid of moonlit figures heralded by the voice of a lover-prophet."

4.5

When I consider recovery, I consider *becoming* as well. I consider what the world lends us, what history no sooner yields to us, what the future asks of us. I consider my entire past, how my family has lived in the American Southwest for eight generations; how their lives were shaped by hope, fear, and love; how they were possibly aggressors and the recipients of aggression. I consider how the countless lives of family members' past have led to the makeup of my own life; how we are all individual brush strokes of a work of art; how we hang on the wall of existence; how we can live and continue to recover in an unjust world. I consider how to write their experiences in a way that justifies my own existence. I consider this my life's meditation.

Try It Yourself(ie): Self-Portrait with Loss

When one thinks of loss, one may think of the many versions of oneself that have gone away, that have transitioned into the past, that have even died, as time moves on. Shedding such versions may be painful, may be a moment of triumph, may be a stage of *becoming* (as we are *all* always in such a stage throughout life). Such shedding may involve freedom from addiction, independence from fear, acknowledgement of an irreparable relationship, or the deep dark after the loss of a loved one.

Whatever the case, the most significant aspect of capturing these feelings is a kind of self-reflection and inquiry that takes deep examination of oneself. The courage it takes is immeasurable. The will it takes to persistently inquire, remarkable. The endurance, nearly too much to bear. In each stage, one loses oneself only to imagine a *new* self. This is where self-elegy for this writer is important. It allows this writer to build anew where destruction once lived.

For this prompt, one should deeply reflect before writing. What is the self that once was that you now lament? What was special about that self? What was frightening? What was the situation that led you to shed that self? What kind of self do you imagine in its place? Why is *self* significant to you? Why is this the right moment for the speaker of your poem to express itself? What does it mean to say, and why? What common ground do you build with the reader? How do you invite them into your poem, so that they see themselves in the poem and the poem in themselves?

Keeper

Today I'm back
in the city where I lived, wondering
what the city keeps, what
of all the muchness
I've called mine.
Skin cells sloughed off,
invisible, mixing
with exhaust and dust.
Hair for a bird's house, breath
that flung itself out
to calla lilies, bougainvillea,
and came back changed:
a different blue, believing.
Blood each month
and more sometimes, when
a knife slipped or I skidded
on shaken pavement, running
the hills I never owned.
Love that returned to me and love
that didn't, spiraling endlessly
somewhere else, and today
it hardly matters
that I don't know where.
Gone so long, I came back wanting
what I missed, each fine grain
that slid or shivered
away, but I can't have again
what's already given, with
or without my knowing.
Now I am spread
in pieces over these streets,

Guerrero and Dolores: warrior,
sad one, shiners
of my bones. Now
I'm telling lemon trees,
the constant plums, I'm
telling you: I lived here
when longing
was the purest thing
I knew, always reaching
for something without heft
or breath that still, I swear,
moves and breathes
in, around, between
each fog-bound house—
where everything is something
I tried to keep, and
couldn't, and can't,
and won't, and won't
stop trying,
with this same heart,
always failing, infinitely lucky
and dumb, and these hands
that keep on
shimmering, wanting
to hold it all.

Robe

You slip it on while, elsewhere,
a painter removes
one object, then another
from each successive sketch.
First: arms through sleeves,
then the belt knotted close.
As first she subtracts the dog beside
the kitchen's open door. Then plates
laid carefully on the table,
the man seated nearby. Trees
outside the window, one by one.
Until only the necessary remains
in the room made itself
by absence. Its cuffs
brush your wrists' tender
skin, the hem lifts
in the slightest shift of air.

The Missing Women

The ones on flyers pinned outside
the pool, papers curling in the chlorinated damp

where I'd wait, after practice,
for my mother, wait to be driven

away. The ones I'd study
over and over—names and faces and *last seen*

wearing, the places they'd disappeared
from. Days my mother came late I couldn't

stop staring, as if by looking hard
their stories would unlock: blue shirt,

bus stop, 1972: I carried them home
then back to the pool, up and down

my narrow lane, the water clear all the way
to the bottom, the slap and reach

of arms and hands—something missing
in me, or something I missed,

as every fall I missed the first leaves
turning, so when I finally remembered

they'd already started letting go,
their vanishing tangling the air.

That season I swam until my fingers puckered,
my still-damp hair, in the parking lot after, stiffened

to clots of ice. I swam and swam and my body
stayed solid, not like the water I knew

it contained. In school we learned how much
of us is liquid, how stories have

a beginning, middle, and an end. I read
of women who turned

to seals in the sea, dove deeper than I could
and came back safe, and I kicked,

turned, pushed away
from the wall, counting laps while the women

knocked inside my head, their weight
buoying me, acolyte of cold,

of split times, lane lines, the secret
history of water. How anyone could slip

from her story like that!—a shape
in paper cut cleanly away. Behind

my shape water sealed
itself shut, somehow I was swimming

into the next day, the next,
into love that seemed sometimes

a desire to be gone, whittled to the thinnest
stem of bone—as those women

might have desired, or not
desired, the ones so lost

by now they must be almost home.

Space for Something Not Yet Known

The more I think about it, the more almost all my poems feel like self-elegies. I didn't consciously create them to be so. But the self that made each particular poem, no matter how close to or far from my life that poem seems, no matter how recent or distant in time—that self is gone, and with it the way of seeing that gave rise to the poem. Each poem is a goodbye to a specific vision. Even if I could return to look at the same tree or bird or length of train tracks, I wouldn't be able to see it in the same way. I'm not the same person who looked that first time and tried to write what she saw. And whatever I looked at would have changed, too. Maybe subtly, but inevitably. There's sorrow in that, and sometimes fear, too—the fear that change often brings. As humans, we love what a Buddhist teacher might call "ground under our feet": something solid and seemingly changeless to stand on. But in submitting to the inevitability of self-elegy, the knowledge that what feels like a permanent self is actually shifting from moment to moment, there's also possibility and hope; there's space where the old self, the old way of looking, used to be. And into that space, anything can come. Anything can happen. It's frightening—and also, exhilarating.

So it seems natural that self-elegies (mine, anyway) might struggle with mixed emotions: anxiety and excitement, grief and hope. "Keeper" feels like a self-elegy that both embraces the term and resists it. In the poem, the losses of self are physical—strands of hair and scraps of skin, blood and breath—and more than physical. There's an irrational hope that the speaker can find the self she used to be—or some part of it—by returning to the place where that self lived. There's a tug between willing relinquishment of self and the stubborn refusal to believe that the old self can't be found again.

In "Robe," the possible conflicting emotions of self-elegy—willingness to let go and reluctance to do so—are less conscious, if they exist at all. The woman in the poem, the "you" it addresses, isn't fully aware of the transformation she's going through. In the background, an artist removes objects and people, one by one, from her work. The woman, living in a parallel world to the artist's, undergoes some sort of change as well, though it's invisible and mysterious. Like the artist's sketch, the woman is "made [herself] / by absence" and loss. Putting on her robe, the woman also somehow lets go of unnamed things, until she's wearing the garment fully and some former self has fallen away. She, like the painter, inhabits a place of absence where what's been taken away has made space for something not yet known.

"The Missing Women" is an elegy that looks outward and inward, mourning both others and the speaker's younger, more hopeful self. The speaker views the missing women of the title with puzzled wonder. From an adult perspective, it's tragically obvious where the women have gone, what has happened to them. But for the child speaker, the women are "almost home," and she too might like to lose herself in order to experience a similar slipping away. The self that is able to see the women's disappearance as strangely magical can't continue past the poem's end: because that self was a child, because the self is always transforming. But there's a longing for that more innocent vision, even so. And maybe, also, a sense that that self still exists in some way, memorialized inside the poem.

Try It Yourself(ie): Weaving Two Strands

Write a poem that weaves together two strands or stories: the first, a description or narrative about your own life; and the second, a description or narrative related to a work of art you love or feel drawn to—another poem, a book, a painting, a piece of music, a dance performance. You might try employing a strict pattern (for example, devoting two lines to "your" story, then two lines to the work of art) or allowing yourself to move back and forth between the two in a more organic way. You could also try playing with point of view—maybe using first or second person to relate the lines about yourself and third person for the lines related to the artwork, or switching this around. Maybe explore verb tense as well, using either the same tense for both strands of the poem or mixing and matching tenses. Try allowing the two strands of the poem to exist side by side without explaining how they're connected; let their relationship arise from the way they live next to each other on the page.

Alchemy

Oceanic gargoyle perched at the spraying
bow of the cumulous ferry. Claws in pockets

chip red sparkle. Home-dyed hair streams
violet. Violent. Destinations wait like strangers'

mouths on dark dancefloors. Say *banality*; she'll tell
you about the crisp letter from the Peace Corps:

Too many issues with food, its crease snapped. It's true
she's lost too many gold rings, forgotten in public rest

stalls. A purging, an attempted exorcism. A rejection
of the world. Say *acuity*; she'll tell you about the nice

lady therapist who told her to give up: *You can't
get milk from the butcher*, she tsked. A gory metaphor

for the girl who refused to *kill two birds with one stone*,
rearranging letters to *feed two birds with one seed*. A bleeding

heart as red as the lipstick she flaunts in airports, hoping
and dreading, re-hoping and re-dreading that someone

will admonish or kiss her. She cannot always tell which.
Or red as the stage lights she needs for the number

with the black feather boa, the white sequined top: *Diamonds,
a girl's best friend*. A purging, a sort of exorcism, an unfurling

confrontation. Defiant-tremulous. Then stalking between
ripped-denim port-goers, sipping a vodka with Diet Coke:

a *skinny bitch*, the bartender says. Least expensive amnesia, calorie-
wise. Say *audacity*; she'll tell you about how the ferry feels

symbolic. *You have to face forward, never backward. That's not
the way you're going.* These arbitrary icepicks we throw at the steep,

the glacial blue of the world. How she stands at the bow
and breathes in the salt, the lashing sideways bluster. How this

is the ultimate exorcist's act—inhaling the broken invisible.
Holding it in one's gargoyle chest. Then spouting it back out as flame.

Falling Three Ways

goodbye to
tombstone eyes and
aubergine nails that scrape the
release,
announcing, *falling—I am a shattered star that*
burrows, upon its descent to the earth; a seed

the girl with
hair down to her waist, whose
porcelain teacup of honey
abruptly
continues to plummet, but
does not extinguish

The Patron Saint of Dinosaurs

The robbers stole your pillowcase. *They must have*
used it as a sack, your father murmurs, holding you. This, the first time

you see him cry. Grandma's pearl ring is gone. The armoire's jaw is busted,
sideways, a cartoon bully with stars around his head. This, your slackened,

loosened home. Records tilt, askew. The neighbors explain
they saw flashlights in the window. *We thought you were playing*

a game, they stammer. *We thought you were telling*
ghost stories. And what is a ghost story? What are its bones? Is this

a ghost story—retelling the glint of the pearl, the birds
on the painted armoire that lifted blue ribbons like blindfolds

coming off? Mom loves to retell the time you sat in a circle
with other preschoolers, confronted the tall guest speaker. A paleontologist

who told a child, *Dinosaurs didn't swim.* How you raised your hand: *Um,*
plesiosaurus did. The finned beast with a swan's curved neck and rows of jutting fangs.

You idolized dinosaurs. Their cavernous skeletons. Notes on things
extinct. Your bedsheets were awash in them—stitched tyrannosaurus rex, gold

triceratops. Stegosaurus with her spine, thorned as a parapet. Merlons,
embrasures alternating, echoing impregnable castle walls. But this is a ghost story

too: a dwelling that cannot be entered. Romanticizing bone reptiles. The notion
that pillowcases have just one use: something easy to rest on.

Distance and Embrace

For me, the self-elegy takes up forgiveness, condemnation, mourning, acceptance, and release all at once. It offers an opportunity to look back on past versions of myself, to confront them and say, through writing, "You are not who I am anymore." There is tremendous power in this. At the same time, writing the poems for this anthology imparted a greater sense of empathy and compassion for those past selves than I had ever felt before. The self-elegy provides a chance to face the past, come to terms with it, embrace it, and thank it, acknowledging that I am still a work in progress. The growth does not stop with the writing of the poem. I recognize that the self I am now may be one elegized by future versions, wiser versions, and there is something humbling and inspiring about that.

Try It Yourself(ie)

Catch What Fell Through the Cracks

"Self-elegy" implies a kind of symbolic death. And indeed, there can be moments where it feels like a part of you dies. But you did survive these moments, and now, you can travel backwards through time in poems to give yourself what you did not have then. Use a poem to catch a piece of you that fell through the cracks during a painful experience. What did you need at that time? What would it have looked like to receive it? If you like, you can create an alter-ego or fictional being who helps you find healing. Write your own mythology: Let the Angel of Manicures take you to the spa, let the Phantom of Muffins treat you to a coffee. What would have helped? Give it to yourself vicariously. Catch what was not caught.

Find Compassion for Yourself

"Self-elegy" also implies the act of grieving. Perhaps that grief comes from the need to mourn a version of yourself that was lost, hurt, or changed against your will. Perhaps it comes from witnessing what stepped in to fill the gaps—a version of yourself driven by trauma, for instance. In a poem, find compassion for yourself in the moments where you wish you would have behaved differently. Grieve the pain that may have been driving you. What would it look like to give your old self permission to grow? To change again for the better? If you like, let your old self speak in the poem. Listen the way no one has ever listened before. End the poem in the spirit of renewal. What would growth look like to you? Give it an image to land on. Give it a shape that feels powerful to you. A spade, a necklace—whatever feels right.

Elegy for the Ambitious Me

You choose to live
in a glass world,
where I've
been hurled from

because life is easier
when you don't care.
I see you—rich as fuck—
and not just with money,

but also with accolades
and art. Maybe I could be you,
but I smash spiders
instead of taking them outside.

That, me,
says it all.

Elegy for the Younger Me

You've already died,
but your phantom hangs around
like the smell of barbecue
or stale garbage.

You see others who have success
and you are proud of them. But,
your phantom face glosses over
as you wonder what could have been.

Envy wraps you like a sheet
with holes popped out for eyes.
You sit next to me while I Netflix
and solidify into a gooey rock.

I turn to you and you to me,
and we want to laugh
but we both know it wouldn't matter.
Maybe one day we will swap places.

I could make a decent ghost.

Devil Dog Road

My grandma used Cheetos
and Capri Suns to bribe me
       to go to church.
We'd sit and stare at things
          and fake religion.
I couldn't stand the smell
         of incense but
       I strangely looked forward to it,
like people often do
         when it comes to strange smells.

After grandma passed away, I dug around
       for photos of her and realized
every time I had posed for a picture
I was reminding someone
in the future that I died.

       Six weeks ago driving through Arizona
I found a road near Flagstaff:
"Devil Dog Road."
Below the sign was a dead golden retriever
         lacquered with flies.
I pulled over and snapped a picture
     because somebody had to.

Question and Answer

1. **Do you see self-elegy as a way to "fix" or justify past experience, maybe find acceptance and/or consolation? How might this work?**

   Answer: For the most part, I see a self-elegy as a way to address multiple identities: the real self and the buried self, or the self that could have been. I find it interesting to think about who I could have been, or who I could become. For the latter, I also think about myself as different identities in terms of how I exist in time. For example, the past, present, and future self. But, the "what could have been" self is really fascinating to reflect on, and considering what you would say to that self is interesting. Ideally, we would not try to seek out acceptance or consolation from elegy, but instead open up the discussion of who we are without judging a version of the self too harshly. Some might choose to use elegy in that way, but I don't see how that approach is fruitful—other than presenting growth, perhaps.

2. **In self-elegies, do you see the self being defined by other—loved ones, objects, obligations, routines, etc.?**

   Answer: As mentioned before, I see the self being defined by identities, whether they are from another time or from an alternate existence. The self is one path of many that we chose to follow—or a path presented to us by circumstance. Either way, we are defined by everything that shapes us, and everything does, in fact, shape us.

3. **In self-elegies, what is lost and/or gained? Can *what might have been or who you might have been* actually be lost? Or inform who you are today?**

   Answer: I think the self-elegy allows meditations on possibility, and that can be interesting, but it can also be a melancholic experience. Usually, what could have been involves some sort of regret or unfulfilled wish. I think what could have been is never lost—the thought never goes away, and writing to the self about it may serve some purpose. As far as informing who you are, who you could have been can inform who you are but it should never dominate who you actually are. We tread in dangerous waters when we shift focus to the "could have been" identity. Maybe there are alternate timelines where we are living the ideal life and made all of the "right" moves, but dwelling on this can be painful.

4. **In self-elegy, to what degree do you see mourning playing a part in re-telling/remembering past selves and/or experiences?**
Answer: I think the amount of mourning depends on how the alternate self is addressed. For example, a younger self may cause the current self to mourn the loss of youth; on the other hand, an alternate self is not necessarily to be mourned if the alternate self is less favorable than the actual self. Even if the alternate self is more favorable, the actual self can find solace in the good/success in its current life. All of this is to say that perhaps, as self-elegies exist in time, they can be used for mourning, but I think they better serve us as a tool for remembering.

Try It Yourself(ie): The Multiverse

Take an event from your life, and make it happen differently in an alternate universe. Then, have your speaker from this alternate universe tell the actual "you" how things could have been. If you're feeling extra adventurous, have another multiverse version of yourself chime in regarding what the event is like in their universe. Think of the butterfly effect. Don't be afraid to make this alternate universe different in multiple ways, not just different versions of yourself, but imagining world events having different outcomes affecting the choices you made and/or the choices your parents or grandparents made.

Unfathered

Suddenly I'm 50 and the bachelor
went to the party without me.
Not only am I my father's age, but
my grandfather's as well, though I'm

no father or grandfather to anyone.
In my 30s, a man who wanted to be
a father asked me to be his partner
in parenting, but I was so young,

so gay—fatherhood was a costume
in a play I would never want
to sit through. Daddy was the man
who paid for my drinks and whose

grey beard nuzzled in my neck,
the stale odors of vodka and Calvin
Kline cologne stayed on the sheets
long after I'd forgotten his name.

In my 40s a woman asked me
to father her children. She also gay,
she with a dream to mother
a brood of half-Black, half-Mexican

babies I could visit any day.
And I said yes. Yes to children
leaving handprints in my living room,
yes to tiny mouths smearing yolk

on my books and milk in my bed.
Yes to the gurgles and cries too
unruly to lock up like toys in a
box. Yes to papa pretense.

I saw myself closer to the men
in my family, to their worries
and joys at having someone
else with whom to spend their

money and their time. I too
wanted someone to grieve
at my loss and to remember me
years after I died. BELOVED

FATHER, prized achievement
engraved on a stone so that
even after death any passerby
would know what I had left

in the broken world. Yet, babies
never came. I walked away
from cradles, baby bottles,
and the badge of honor

memorialized on my grave.
Sometimes I visit that
cemetery. A bright bouquet
of flowers—marigold, myrtle,

and baby's breath—an offering
to the father I might have been,
but also to the father I never had.
How I yearned for his approval

and affection. How I've walked
the lonely earth and will continue
walking still, mourning the men
too improbable to be true.

To the Old Man Who Sits on the Horizon

Only yesterday you seemed far away.
Today you're so close I can sense your
breathing, incarnate silhouette much clearer
than the day before. Your ears as crisp

as butterflies newly sprouted from their
bone cocoons. I look back at my younger self
and marvel at everything I left behind
with him: my fear of loneliness, of aging,

of falling asleep and not finding my way
to daylight again. Abuelo mourned his teeth
more than he cried over the loss of his legs.
Gone were the kitchens of his ecstasy

and the tasty slaughter of pulsing meats.
The line-up of small spice jars stares from
a distance like headstones people have
ceased to visit. Abuela, out of pity, stuck

a piece of corn tortilla in his mouth
and Abuelo nearly choked to death,
but that was the last flavor of home
he would ever dissolve on his tongue.

Was it cruel to remember what once
had meaning? Was it more valuable now
that it was gone? By the time I take
a seat beside you I will know. Old man,

what do you still hold in your hands?
My father kept a bottle of beer—his
loyal companion present during the births
of his children and the demise of his wife.

He perched it, like a bird, on his knee.
When the sun was about to set he let

the bird go but it had long forgotten how
to be free. It sank into the sand, becoming

the widower my father used to be, with
puckered lips going dry, yearning for a kiss.
I'm in the stretch of the journey when I
get to decide what stays nestled inside

the cradle of my fingers: the book
I never finished? my wedding ring,
the only vestige of a two-year marriage?
an alebrije from Oaxaca, reminder of

a paradise that scattered a trail of stars
each night to ensure her children's safe
return? Your shoulders tremble, old
man. It must feel cold to sit exposed

on the horizon where even the ocean
and the sky look flat and clenchable
like photographs. Old man, you're not
shivering, but laughing. I can't wait to find

the humor in a lifetime of sorrow and pain.
It must be liberating to chuckle at the fools
right behind you, slowed down by the weight
of their pasts when peace is within reach.

Reckoning with Absence

I turned fifty during the pandemic. I bought a small chocolate cake and ate half of it as three of my closest friends watched via Zoom. They too had turned fifty earlier in the summer, so I was the last to join the club. I attempted to engage them in deep conversation about what happens next and if we were satisfied with what happened already, but they didn't seem interested. The platform was all wrong, and one of my friends had a terrible Internet connection that kept freezing her image in the most awkward and distracting poses. I left it alone and resorted to small talk.

Not at all how I wanted to mark that milestone. My plans to celebrate my birthday on a Greek island, sipping wine and waxing poetic on my past achievements while watching the ocean wrestle with the gorgeous beach was not meant to be. Instead, I sat on my balcony and looked out at the empty Newark streets, a bottle of Prosecco at my feet. Perhaps it was the state of the world in July 2020 that plunged me into a deep depression.

I had been in isolation for four months, and there were many more to come. The loneliness was unbearable, particularly when I recognized that my books and awards were not keeping me company. Looking at the past made me solemn and remorseful. I had made life decisions that had secured my professional career but not my personal life. Was it worth it? Was it worth crying about it now? These are not very original questions, but how we negotiate them is unique to each person.

In the poems I wrote during the summer of the pandemic, I wanted to come to terms with the loss of the person I could have been had I made different choices. But I also wanted to make peace with the choices I had made but now regretted. And finally, because I was arriving at an age that my father and grandfather had reached before me, I wanted to feel a connection to the men who lead by both good and bad example. The self-elegy is complex that way: it is not only a reckoning with absence, it is also a reckoning with what came, for better or for worse, to inhabit that vacant space.

Try It Yourself(ie): Reckoning with Absence

During a pandemic, how do we come to terms with the loss of the person we could have been had we made different choices? How do we make peace with the choices we made but now regret? Write a poem about your pandemic birthday, what it was like and what it could have been under different circumstances. Include the good and bad, include the individuals in your life that led by both good and bad examples. Let your self-elegy be a "reckoning with absence" and with what came, for better or for worse, to inhabit that vacant space and then became you.

Self-Portrait at Eighteen Seen at Thirty

Let me rinse your blue hair cut
your bleached tips and butter
your scalp with balm from the pharmacy
they'll call the cops if you show
so I'll foot the bill I'll drive
the Lincoln since it's past 10:30
I'll clean the pillow you ruined
writing violets purple martins with dye
and restlessness the landscape
of your sleep mapped here
hang onto one of these
honor it like a flag and
burn it when you turn twenty-one
these love letters won't mean much now
sorry in advance for the bloody seam
on your left thigh see how it winds
like a garden snake halved with a hoe
sorry for how badly it hurts
to watch the next one in your rearview
I don't want to give anything away
but here's a pencil and some paper
here's a box of Kleenex and a laptop
full of porn I recommend the chicken
ginger let me walk you to your car
you're drunk where are your keys
later when you write all this down
those are narcissus those are egrets
the word you're looking for
is *pobrecita* the phrase you mean
to write is *I know now I will love*
which isn't false but let's get you

presentable boy because we only
have twelve years to break you open
leave you in a ditch somewhere
and see what crawls out

Chemo

The man dreams of a waterpark
a boy with a tube splashes

in an artificial river what a day
he's having what a lark

raising the water in baptism
over daddy late summer

light searches clavicle pelvis
the father's worried hands

in the clam-shaped tide pool
everyone is having fun

and no one forgets his father's
suitcase at the nurse's station

the sun-sweet clouds tussle over
the boy and his father until

the waves shunt them apart
send the father ahead so the boy

bobs distantly behind him
in the water's course like the tail

of a puppy now the boy wails
joyous with the thrill

of gravity's pulse and
the father you can see it

by his darting eyes
is worried to go over the drop ahead

is worried to let the child second him
but the boy is just a wavelet yet

and so many others already
wait in the tide pool

so what's to worry
incendiary blaze tinges

his hairy chest his bald head
the machine roar

of the churning swill
he plunges *goodbye*

daddy shouts the boy
goodbye!

One Need Not Be a Coward to Die a Thousand Deaths

"Acoward dies a thousand times before his death" says Shakespeare's Julius Caesar. But truth be told, one need not be a coward to die so many deaths; so much of each person passes away before the light fades from their eyes. It is no surprise then that writers seek to eulogize those parts of themselves they have lost: their beauty, their naivete, their rage, their dogmas, their leniencies, their shunned or shelved selves. To attempt to name and mourn these former selves is the act of self-eulogy.

As an undergraduate, I studied history. I poured over the stories of gulag survivors, recorded narratives of native tribes now gone, and investigated the lives of women whose historical selves are mere caricatures of their living incarnations. History records, but it also reduces. I find myself pushing against the reductiveness of history by embracing double entendre, resisting the teleology of punctuation, and considering the reactivity (in all its meanings) of a poem's final word. Through this lens, I hope to create a visage of the self, which, like Caesar, is complex, problematic, and worthy of not just tears, but serious consideration.

Try It Yourself(ie): Tragic Core

Write a poem that is an address to yourself at a much younger age. Include details that would be immediate for your former self, perhaps specific objects or locations significant to that former self. What advice would you offer about work, about life, about relationships? What advice might they offer you? What would be the tone of the conversation? Consider making a tragedy or mistake at the core of the poem. Never mention the tragedy directly, but hint at it throughout the text. Consider why the speaker withholds this information. What can your poem say without saying it?

Elegy for the Selves

What am I afraid of?
Everything flares up.

A star explodes,
traffic merges

into one lane.
The points of a star

nudge me in my sleep.
Wake up, weak lamp.

I come to, blink
in spots. A cloud offs

into a tree, a tree
sloughs off its leaves.

A leaf turns in the dark
and it is your back.

*

Death sits among
my things.

A dresser opens and
a mosquito flies out.

The sky above is full
of seeds, falling.

Each morning, watermelons
huddle in a market.

My grandfather bites
into a slice slowly.

The sun sloshes above.
A truck covers the sound

of the bite, the bite
covers the simmering sky,

the tired leaves on
the tired ground.

*

I carry these selves
everywhere.

How an ox carries
a family across

a flood, its bell
submerged and whistling

to and fro. I have
this habit of pouring

out *just so*. Water
in the dip of my roof,

mosquitos stretching
forth their legs,

thinned by wind
or thinned to waste

my crueler self.

*

Ants tunnel through
plum glow. Legs stuck

in heart, meat of
my sweeter self.

Twilight spreads a museum
of flies circling

my mother's wrist, a bracelet
of wings and eyes.

Too far to see, I threw
a horseshoe at no

particular stake
and it wrung

a neck. Fearless,
my little amp of a head,

resounding off.

*

Flour covers my face
and I laugh to be

a ghost. I let loneliness
slide through me,

kin to slug and
kind to no other.

I strike stone to stone
to make every fire

in every building.
This is self-love,

as we are taught.
The eye of an eel

my father turns on a spit,
rolling in my mouth.

It was summer
when I killed the first

self. The fire did
its work and left

nothing to see but
all to spark.

Lessons on Lessening

I wake to the sound of my neighbors upstairs as if they are bowling.

And maybe they are, all pins and love fallen over.
I lay against my floor, if only to feel that kind of affection.

What I've learned, time and again:
Get up. You can not have what they have.

And the eyes of a dead rat can't say anything.

In Jersey, the sink breaks and my mother keeps a bucket
underneath to save water for laundry.

A trickle of water is no joke. I've learned that.
Neither is my father, wielding a knife in starlight.

I was taught that everything and everyone is self-made.

That you can make a window out of anything if you want.
This is why I froze insects. To see if they will come back to life.

How I began to see each day: the sluice of wings.
Get up. The ants pouring out of the sink, onto my arms in dish heavy
    water.

My arms: branches. A swarm I didn't ask for.

No one told me I'd have to learn to be polite.
To let myself be consumed for what I can not control.

I must return to my younger self. To wearing my life
like heavy wool, weaved in my own weight.

To pretend not to know when the debtors come to collect.

Always Coming of Age

I came of age, then, in the Dream House, wisdom practically
smothering me in my sleep. Everything tasted like an almost
epiphany. — Carmen Maria Machado, *In the Dream House*

In thinking about my past, present, and future selves, I think about wisdom: "I must return to my younger self. To wearing my life / like heavy wool, weaved in my own weight." I think about what my five-year-old self knew then, what she might have said to her father who disappeared once again in Atlantic City. Maybe she said: *you're not supposed to go*. Maybe she stared at him so hard, he turned into a pool of butter and stayed that way.

I am always coming of age. I am always with and without my selves. In acknowledging my many selves, I find comfort; I find that "self-love, // as we are taught." My selves have undergone trauma, have had men grasp at their necks. These past selves never leave me. In healing, in poetry, they grow new wings, new songs. My twenty-seven-year-old self collapses beside a door, always closed; today, I feed her a cornucopia of avenues, of open oceans. My selves are ancestral: tied to my mother, my grandmother, my great-grandmother, and so on. In the earlobes and palms and strands of hair we share, I celebrate each iteration.

Try It Yourself(ie): Wisdom to a Younger Self

Return to your younger self. What would your younger self tell you now? What wisdom would you offer yourself? What did you know back then? What have you learned about truth or beauty or morality or other abstract ideas we often take for granted? How has this knowledge changed in the in between years? Try speaking directly to this younger version of yourself. Turn this into a poem.

To Claim Where I Am

In this state of in-between is both silence and   the screech of longing

Asked daily to get over their mistakes made in ignorance
Never ready with bated breath answers for the questions they ask
or with stories prepared to remind them of what they already know
Worked hard to forget friction of desire to feel understood
To persist in a vacuum of belonging

Instead, a melody of music is what I pin my hopes on
That someday, somewhere, someone will just sit back and listen
Let my chorus of voices reclaim the multitude of ways to yearn, grieve,
rejoice

Cause amongst my ribs, spleen and heart
I live in an emptiness crowded by caterpillars inching in determined
directions
I nurse wounds which, when kindled, ignite baggage from the past
I make room for ancestors who slaughtered each other, who ran from deci-
mation, who benefited from annihilation

This body born backwards, turning inside out
spills menstrual blood onto the carpet
lurches as movement, demands change just to get in the door
is still unsure how to protect the bits exposed

In between sacrifice and gift
I make a home in
a canyon which leads only back into itself
through spiral, circle, rocky existence
It makes sure
I learn everything's name, as part of my name
this canyon which claims me, teaches me patience
a kind of truth without resolution

A Self-Elegy in Four Parts

1. This is an elegy for the ways my beauty fails to be understood
For the people afraid to take truth in for fear of their own vulnerability
They believe my birthright a lifetime of mourning body
Politely name it:
> Battle
> Inspiration
> Overcoming who I am

2. I claim disabled
> When their response is, *"I'm sorry,"* I tire of explaining
> This used to bug me the most, their apologies for my existence
> Kindness masked as fear is dangerous
> Genocide always first justified by difference

3. Freedom was when I tore my eyes from the mirror
> Realized reflection can never capture moon during eclipse
> So much more than quiet shadow
> When I gaze down at navel, I am awed by brilliant light
> Dissonance between who I am and how I am seen

4. This is the grieving song for the corporeal appetite of productivity and
attractiveness
> The arbitrary measurements tallied to makes up the value of a person
> This is my own anguish that no amount of effort, proves I am human

Untitled

Failure as
        an activist
        artist
Not for lack of trying
           Writer
           who forgets words
           who can't spell
           who has no idea how to   say it right
                                          make it clear
                                          Tires of pushing
                                          Doesn't know the flow if
                                          it drowned her in a torrent of
                                          creative enlightenment

      Scared

Tired of being afraid

(She was NEVER a coward
She who hit the kid in preschool who made fun of her
Refused to apologize
She who doesn't know
anything other than being
a fighter
She knew when she was not sorry)

--Rip here---

I can't tear off parts
of myself
Shed the messy bits like unwanted skins
Even as pieces may float to the bottom
where do they go?

Playa Revuelta

to be needed
to be black sheep
to be pulled back
        forced to stay behind
to be controlled by judgment
to be mocked different
to be shamed for the facts

        scrape, grind, my surfaces raw
        reveal what I am made up of

        changed by external forces
        exposed eventually

to be sand
how does one varnish that which wears, strips, decomposes

to be a rock in water
buff me smooth
shine me by blunt force trauma
make me perfectly round
no more snag, stuck, ensnare
roll on, too many stories to tell

Self-Elegy to Borders

In the US-MX borderlands, I have lived the permeability of boundaries and experienced the in-between spaces many folks would much rather remain walled off and separate. Sitting on gritty dirt between a dazzling array of cacti thorns, I've observed butterflies migrating across the line and lizards burrowing underneath.

There's a part of me that wishes that my nine-year-old self had this knowledge when I was parked in place in my manual wheelchair, stranded on the asphalt blacktop near the gate to the playground. As a racially mixed kid, this is where I spent a fair amount of time answering the question, "What are you?" from kids impatiently loitering, waiting to duck out of the heat back into the classroom. As a disabled kid, I also spent a lot of time fielding the question, "What's wrong with you?" Squirming under the bright light of desert sun and expectant eyes, I learned no one likes nuance.

Trying to answer the question, "What's wrong with you?" had its complications. I could rattle off the unintelligible name of my disability, but that never seemed to satisfy. It only seemed to prompt the question, "But what *happened* to you?" Like there had to be some reason for my joints, muscles, and body's shape being so different than their own. I felt embarrassed for not having the words they seemed to so desperately need. Ashamed because they obviously saw the way I was as bad, as a consequence to something terrible having happened. There was no way to explain that away.

As blunt and harsh as kids can be, they left me at a very tender age grappling with the stories I tell about myself.

There were a lot of racially mixed kids in my class, but this was way before identity politics made its way to my neighborhood, and I lacked the language to give a succinct and short answer. I grappled with not just my story, but how my story was interwoven with my family's story as documented and undocumented immigrants. There was a legacy which trailed after us of what was left behind and what expectations were and were not met. By trying to unravel what this all meant, it's no surprise I ended up in activism work as a late teen.

One warm summer evening at a conference in a very green and tree-filled Minneapolis, I was discussing the question of, "What are you?" with a racial justice activist whose answer was that I was going to have to choose. They were assuming, of course, that there was only two parts of my cultural identity to choose from. They exerted that I better get clear about how the world was going to see me and that was the identity I should pick.

I spent the next decade of my life trying to answer this riddle, until I realized this riddle was uncrackable. I wanted to acknowledge all of who I was. To own the privilege from being light-skinned, but also recognize the utter confusion I experienced with social norms and rules in predominantly white, colonial spaces. To make space for the cultural and ancestral knowledge peeled from my familial skin by both forced and chosen migration, as well as by the direct annihilation of some of my ancestors on the land they lived on for generations. To have the violence and dynamic beauty of living on the border understood in the context of familial pride and shame. I wanted to have language, at least for myself, for the friction which left me raw with the effort of trying on masks to represent myself to a world which desired borders built and body truth contained.

In the past, as now, these questions follow me everywhere I go. I cannot sit in a group of people, no matter the place, or age range, without questions about what I am inevitably coming up. Now whenever someone asks me some kind of version of, "What's wrong with you?" I have well-worn answers—"I'm disabled." To which they certainly respond with some version of, "Yeah, but what *happened* to you." I respond, "I don't disclose my diagnosis, because to me, disability is a social and political identity." This answer contains too much nuance. This is when people make up their own answers. "My kid has XYZ but she can't get around nearly as well as you do." "My sister is (their uncomfortable pause) *differently-abled* like you, and she lives in a group home." I learned that the stories I tell don't matter much. People ask these questions from a place of grappling with what I reflect to them versus who I actually am. My stories exist for me.

Self-elegy, to me, is a wrestling with nuance, the complicated stuff that is not easily packaged or explained. Digesting the grief of never being seen, the layers unconsumable. Self-elegy, is an evolution of goodbyes to how I understand my internal universe. The epic journeys of delving deeper only to realize I was digging a grave for the way I understood previous selves. This mourning is both a letting go and a reclamation. It is also a journey I don't take alone, but one which happens in the context of my relationships, family, neighborhood, and community.

Finding my way as a young adult to community activist spaces, I observed how limited we humans are dealing with the stuff between—right or wrong, fight or fail, and all of the dichotomies that we judge ourselves by. I watched people burnout and leave. Beautiful, thoughtful people who lived in multiple worlds like me. As I buckled under exhaustion, I realized that this lifetime of living between the lines was a skill. That embracing subtle shifts was one way to embody a practice of self-care. I wrote about this for activists, interviewing folks all over the country, but I also wanted to share my story.

I wrote pages and pages about identity, culture, and my stories of navigating around other people's confusion. None of it was right. Ready to give up, I finally went to my poet self. She thrives on nuance and doesn't have to have the perfectly concise answers. I asked her how she would explain my story. She replied, "*I was born with four names. Four names to interlace my mind, body, intuition, and spirit. Each name, like the four directions, weaves the whole of who I am. This woven existence is against The Rules*" (Ortiz 2018, 19).

Each self-elegy I find the song for, also contains a never satiated grief for society's desire, and expectation, that I will build borders, walls, and vigilantly monitor parts of myself to prevent any complication of understanding. My poet self gently takes my hand and reminds me that my world is about mending. Because if the people pestering me with questions aren't gonna *get it*, at least my truth can make sense to me.

Try It Yourself(ie): Friction Between Self and World

Do you find yourself "in between" worlds? What is a story you tell yourself about an area of friction between yourself and the world? Are there components of this story that no longer feel true? Why or why not? What ways do you deflect the assumptions of others? Do you grapple with nuance in your poetry? In other creative expressions? How so? What are specific concrete images for frictions, or possibilities, created by being "in between" worlds?

Multiple Timelines and Selves

A poem is specific to one occasion, one way of seeing; the moment passes, and the poet changes, becomes someone new. The poet will never interpret the occasion exactly the same way again.

These ever-changing moments make up our ever-shifting identities. Can multiple selves exist at the same time, multiple timelines with each possible path stemming from one small choice that both negates and creates new versions of self, versions branching off with each step? If so, even when choices are negated by actions, or by a failure to take action, those almost-selves still influence identity. Whether or not we are aware of that influence is where self-elegy and agency come into play; in this section, the poets included treat past selves a little like Schrödinger's cat—both alive and dead until unwrapped and confronted, embraced or rejected.

Postcard Divinations

1. The Archaic Frame of Body

Bone as an exhalation of form

   glass stained by glass

Time as a mirror of negation

   no help in the heap of surrender

Home as a parlor of fish

   the yard in your world in duress

Words are unfavorable to infinity

   we could not have known what leaving would mean.

2. A Charge of Wildness Crashing into a Paper Tree

She became a teller of screams.

Fell away into a halo of keys.

A nest can be a shallow depression in sand, a burrow in the ground, a chamber in a tree, an enormous pile of seaweed, a mud dome with an entrance tunnel.

3. The Shell of a Shadow in an Egg

Saint Ann is the patron saint of horseback riders and doors.
She asked, "Please, tell me what this means?"

4. Middle Visitation

A poet's mouth in the statue's mouth.

You cannot go back to a point of origin

placing elegant patterns in cadaverous replica.

Nostalgia looping around her voluptuary:

talismanic, skeletal.

The marble forceps pulling.

> But when I saw her molecules cascade—
> I wanted—it didn't matter how near or far—
> to touch them like skin.

5. ci vediamo

From different parts of the world. Her three-dimensional bay
of altars made language stampede.

"I am an old woman," she said, "you must come back soon."
The dark purple octopus: its pride of tentacles on my tongue.

Our Sicilian fishing port no longer maps.
Her quadrant of arms is my new nautilus.

The cloud was a fin or a brain therefore I returned.
The seam of not touching.

I often wanted

to lift her in the air,

lift and lift.

Pray Her Leather Bracelet

She lay down with her, she laid with her
as a mark of separation within the sentence.

"You don't look like yourself anymore."
"Let me take a photograph. It will look more like *you*."

She painted a yellow bird and made curtains out of what was left.
It all became an odd house.

Iron the grieving clothes. Pack. Unpack.
Pray her leather bracelet makes her happy in the name of.

"I kissed a Madonna today. She kissed me back. We slept together. I stayed and stayed." I said, "Her strength was a contraction, an inhalation, a continuous forgiveness of failed empathy. A thunderous stanzaic penumbra until she moved and I ran." She said, "No, wait. I will wait. You are everywhere whether you are here or not here. Waiting is the same as not waiting." I said, "In absentia, you. What about you? The design strips the body communing. People do not talk like this. I will learn to draw eyes. Focus would be the color on which this is printed." She said, "Here are six books on perspective. That is the hardest. The vanishing point."

The Name of This Essay Changes Everyday

"In the beginning" "of the world" "there was a whole" "edgeless
entity," "sea of dreaming," "of floating" "changeable shape"
"After a while" "was differ-" "rentiation," "as if pieces of sea,"
"of water," "became fish" "As if air" "became birds —" "I can't
remember"–Alice Notley

When I first began thinking about self-elegy, I was reading Alice
Notley's, *The Descent of Alette*, which compelled me to consider
deeper facets of story, voice, mythology and time: the creation
of a creation myth, beginnings and endings. The stanza above kept return-
ing to me in the day, in the night. It felt sad and gorgeous: the re-emergent
feminist body, devastation, radical solace, animism, shapelessness. There was
a convergence and immersion. I had been writing about the direct and intri-
cate experience of grief and the subsequent loss of a known self.

During that time, I lost six significant family members and dear friends in-
cluding my mother and sister in just a few months. After that, the membrane
of self was gone, and the reach of poetry became mazelike. It felt as though
I was chasing the specter of absence. I saw it turn both me and my work as
unrecognizable. It was a strange beholding of pain that I experienced and
witnessed at the same time, a disorienting personification of self.

Consequently, it was impossible to reflect on a definition of self-elegy
without tending to the resonance of continuous bereavement. The distur-
bance of poetics was spectacular. My writing changed. My writing practice
changed. I disappeared. I reappeared. I couldn't read. I could read. I lost the
illusion of the reassurance of language. Reconstructing a self, reconstructing
a poem was a misshapen wilderness. I couldn't feel it for a really long time.

Questions such as how to write about grief and empathy, without dis-
sipating into an exhausting nostalgia, became curious and unanswerable.

The self, in a line, on the page fell away. Yet, it takes both an acuity of self and selflessness to write poetry. In this aesthetic conversation, patience and compassion as much as the hard work of art, I think, are part of a complex definition of self-elegy.

I had, many years before, been given the diagnosis of laryngeal dystonia, a neurological condition which impedes the production of speech. My physical connection to language changed dramatically. A hyper-awareness of verbal exchange, at first, undermined interaction. Words became a self-closing mechanism, an involuntary striation of voice-breaks that could sometimes upend vocalized and written words. It has been anomalous since then—more fraught and fragmented—while, at the same time, a different, more relational and beautifully collaborative way of working emerged.

The potentially sentimental sense of my given voice as a lost "being"— in speech and in poetry—is not a viable ballast, yet I find that it is almost unthinkable not to look toward or attempt to engage with a sound-scape or self-scape that is no longer available.

For me, literal and metaphorical death or silence now co-exists in the same body and the same embodied page, its ongoing incubation and iteration. I try, but I am unable to conceive of self-elegy as a discrete, literary subgenre. I think of it as a multiplicity, as being genre-less: not limitless, but nuanced and un-demarcated as if the poetics of self/voice that I have lost can never be separate from what I might create now: *as if birds became air.*

9 Meadowview Road

That summer my sister thought she knew
she was taking acid but not four

hits of it and slithered in her snakeskin
from bed to floor, I learned how to hide.

I hid under my desk, in my closet.
I hid in the branches of an apple tree.

I hid in the kitchen inside the black
letters of my favorite books. My best

friend in the neighborhood
put on the lipstick of a stranger.

My neighborhood—three small lanes
of clotheslines and peek-through

windows. I learned to swallow
the morning fog for breakfast, to eat

pine needles for lunch. Running
through the overgrown field behind

my house, running to my new
best friend the library with its heavy

quiet. Fiction books that smelled
of my mother's bureau drawers.

My sister thought she was slipping
on more of her adult skin.

I thought I was running
further toward home.

The Ornithologist Searches for a Shared Ancestry

I sought only the slow discoveries when I was young,
allure of the yellow caterpillar, sign of a cosmic self, I thought.

If I felt myself without direction, I consulted the ruffle
of the ranunculus, the metabolism of willow flycatcher.

I sought self-ness in my teapot. Called it self-nests.
Practiced opacity while watching wagtails and pipits.

I calibrated my hunger by the rigorousness of the seagull's
thrust to my thrown french-fry. My thirst to the thrum of hummingbird's

skull. Were my yearnings flimsy tiny parachutes I flung in my back
yard? Some suffocating grid of circumvention? There is no current

evidence to suggest a common ancestor, I heard the wood thrush sing.
I am an accidental species species species, I sang back.

Abandoned Girl is Full of Words

but doesn't know how to speak them.
She feels *shimmer* in her shin bone
green in every breath she sips
ululation carefully as it buzzes her
like tequila-on-fire. The peonies
have such a power: *frill* & *petal*
sepal & *stem.* Cup in her hand presses
pottery & *shard, blaze* & *kiln* into her fingers.
How to speak of this to others?
The breeze carries *hemispheres* & *maps*
sirocco & *tailspin* & *mistral* which moves
into *mist* and *ministry* and there is her grandfather
and *grandfather clock* and *time* and then *ticking* and *stick* and
and you are talking to her and she
cannot speak of it.
How dumb she appears to you. How mute.

Curating the Self

In thinking about what makes certain poems self-elegies, and what that means to me, I believe that the word *creation* is key. So many people talk about *curating* their selfies on Facebook. To me, that has a superficial quality, a literal face value placed upon our moments, with the emphasis always on which picture makes the poster look the best. When I am creating a poem about something that has been lost within me, whether my childhood or a love, I am trying to achieve more complexity—an insight into the me that was part of that loss, and which will bring more understanding to the self that is in the moment of writing the poem. But then, if I am honest with myself, am I not also curating myself in these poems? What do I choose to emphasize, what do I choose to delete, or let stay unpublished? What I hope for is more complexity with the self-elegy than with a selfie. Perhaps something that was unclear to me at a moment in childhood renders itself slightly more in focus or more palatable for me.

With a selfie, complexity is difficult to add in. For example, here is a picture of me biking with my son, showing to the world one of the moments when I am feeling like a good mother. Perhaps just out of range of that picture, I have scolded my son, or been impatient with him. I doubt I will remember that in a selfie, or that you can see it. But when I write a poem about being a mother, I can write about more than how I am in one moment. I contain all the moments that I have been up to now, but I will choose to write about this moment and then this moment, and so on. I can write about the bad mother times along with the good mother times, too, all in the space of a poem. This adding up of moments then is one concept of time. I cannot help but feel that time is just another dimension of myself. That time is of me. The future is how the future will affect me, until I die. Then time will of course cease to exist. Just for me. And in this way, I manage time in my poems. As a writer, I get to tell myself what has happened to my previous self in ways that make it more interesting to me. Which brings me to another element, the fictional me.

"The Ornithologist Searches for a Shared Ancestry" is obviously a creative fictional poem. I did not have a clear back and forth with a wood thrush. But birding was an important part of my childhood so an element of this has a truth to it. A fictional truth. One that has brought me an understanding of myself—I do feel like an accidental species at times in my life. I'm sure we all do. But that moment lets me tell it to my previous self and comforts the me that is now. This is such a bonus of self-elegies—that I can live my life over again, but in slightly different ways. This moment happened, yes, but what if I add this element to it? Or if I bring in this image, what happens to that moment—how or will it expand out to now? Reincarnation through creative curation.

I guess I'm not sure what a self-elegy is. Or how it works in my poems. I do know that writing about my past lets me relive it in a different mood or emotional framework than I was in at the moment, which is usually confusion: why is this happening right now the way that it is happening? But when I'm writing a poem, time works differently in me: I lose track of it because I'm so invested in the past. And when I'm writing a poem, the past works differently. And who knows? Maybe if I find a small truth, this poem will work on my future differently, too. When I get there, I hope I'm writing a poem to find out and report back.

Try It Yourself(ie): List Yourself

For your self-elegy, make a list of some of the hobbies you and your family did together. It can be something like walking the dog, car trips to your grandparents, a family vacation. Then make a list of images from your childhood home, like what your room looked like, where you ate dinners, your basement, and so on. Then make a list of images or words that are currently your favorite. Write a poem about a memory from the list of the hobbies you did with your family and try and incorporate images from both lists and see if you can create a moment from your past that stays true to that past but adds an element of where you are now. On revision, see if you can transpose something you've learned about yourself and insert it into the past.

from The Science of Impossible Objects

dear imaginary daughter,

There is no heat of you moving beneath my skin, no heartbeat knocking the inner machinery. But the halogens have been flickering for weeks, bees in all the sockets. Honey in all the spaces no one has licked. Even at night, my fingers grow slick with figs, my rabbit purse fallen open on the bed. Lewdly, sticking my fingers where they don't belong. Boredom is a tangible thing, heavy, like a bed or a suitcase we've tossed everything into that wasn't on fire. Downstate, I keep wearing shoes that blister my heels, the water rising to the surface where anything rubs too hard or just hard enough. It was always like this, sunburned, each summer, my hair going green at the bottom of the pool. The heat chafing my inner thighs. A mess of biology and awkwardness. But listen to them when they say the trauma of previous generations exists in your infrastructure. Drunk grandmothers and slutty aunts. The twin you may or may not have eaten in the womb stalking you from the other side of the door.

dear imaginary daughter—

When you're born, we both go pink with light. Dream dark and sparkling and full of stars. I try to keep you safe in the box of my body, but you escape. Skate the backyards, play *Sweet Mary Mack* with neighborhood kids, but still your eyes go black with neglect. Amazingly, you still marvel at ability to hide twilight under the hem of my skirt. We make a game of it, here then gone, then here again. This body so heavy, like a cold, dead moon. On my knees in the coat checkroom, there was so much blood, we made an ocean of it. As if *ocean* were a verb, we *oceaned* into being. I make crashing noises with my mouth while they sort out the carnage. A life dividing again and again, shooting off in all directions.

Defining Legacies

I've often heard people talk about their experiences in raising children as an impetus to either revisit their own childhoods, or perhaps, more often, to undo their childhood. To revise their own history and recreate it knowing now what they or their parents might not have known then. As someone child-free by choice, this idea fascinates me. How then does the childless woman, existing in a world where so much of her "value" exists in her ability to spawn children, navigate this? What do we, whatever gender, lose in that revisiting and undoing? Are there other ways of wrestling with those issues without parenthood? Does art work in the same way?

The beginnings of this project were a Pinterest page where a woman was outfitting an entire fictional child with clothes and accessories with funny captions. What are children (especially fictional ones we seem to have more control over) but a reflection, in some way, of their parents—reflection of their parent's DNA, mannerisms, personalities. Even art is similar. Our writing a reflection of our influences, our passions. But also has a life outside of us and away. You could then say every child is a work of art, even the actual ones, that eventually leave us and go out and navigate their own way in the world.

Late last year, my own mother passed away, and the situation of being motherless made me think a lot about what it means to be a daughter, and as a result, to return to this particular project that was sort of languishing unfinished. If we are the sum product of our parents' genetics and experience, the nature and the nurture, how much of our personality is really, undeniably our own? If we are works of art, when we go out into the world, how much of what we say, what we think, how we see things belongs to us?

And if we in turn, we do not go on to have our own children, what is lost? How do we compensate for that as artists?

Try It Yourself(ie): Nonexistent You

Write a letter to an imagined, but nonexistent version of yourself or another person. Who do you think you could have been? Think of a path not taken, a choice not made. Think of who you might be if a crucial moment in your life had turned out differently. How might you look at love, hate, friendship, betrayal differently? How is this "you" different? List contradictions. Talk directly to this other "you." Turn this into a poem.

A Mental Vision of a Series of Events (Florida)

I.

I am your panorama, standing in the still fog covering
the sleek asphalt as it merges with the lake fronts. Here
the rain is afterthought to this humidity. Another burning humility.
If I could I would cover the water in thin sheets of thought—
lay down my metaphorical coat for you to cross. But this
isn't it, this is an insult. We started in a perfect space, &
now all this time, all this distance we have overcome. We stop
in a panhandle hotel with broken ice

machines & cheap soap & odors we must chose not
to identify. I stare down at our bags, imprecise fragments
of this life we fought so hard for. I know you look to me to be all your
colors & to be our ship's manifest. But I am also our witness to original
intentions, & to all of those colors we had to ignore.
I stand weary, trying to hold my breath as the clouds push down upon me.

II.

I meant to start a poem about you &
how the landscape always shapes us
even when we think we are shaping
ourselves. Then this sinking feeling
happened, this floundering of words.
Words with no direction. They were
angry words with little meaning & now
only a warm rain to show for it.

I shifted my position in the front seat
of the moving truck, thought of how easy
it would be for me to complicate us, this move, this stretch-
ing of our path into your future. I quelled
myself, turned on a Simon & Garfunkel song, &
thought of America as *our* landscape, *our* place of forgotten transitions.

III.

Tell her, I was somebody else's panorama
back in 1987 when it was
okay to lie or at least to fake & so
all the colors were mine & maybe
they were yours, too. You may have
given up; I transitioned. Old Polaroids
give us our details, mini-obelisks to mark
our memory spots. A reckoning is

overdue, & even as I raise another glass I know
my imbalance cannot be set right by repetition.
For a moment I long to kiss you from
the photograph, to caress you from this distance with
the back of my hand, the part that still tingles when I touch you.
The colors bleed together & I wince.

IV.

No narration, just the humid facts
of another Florida night & the rustling
of unpacked boxes under refrigerated
air. *So little is hidden between us now.*
If we can, we will unpack them all
in the days to come. The stillness
in your stare that used to frighten all
my marijuana selves finally begins

to recede, a bong cloud dissipating high
above these lines. The doors to our new place
latch us together & so much depends
on our resilience now that I can't
back down. I'll pretend that holding on
is a sign of life, & blame the sky that let me follow.

V.

I won't lie. I crawled through
those years after we sent my mother away. My pot
haze gave me an excuse for fracturing
an already *brokenness*. The fire station
we left her at is a motif in all my night-
mares, & a future I wait for, one that I know I belong
to. It's okay, I slipped passed the outer swords

of our marriage civility, when I thought we
might be able to talk someday. I know I am no longer
your panorama. Were it that I could be a part
of those colors, remain in the wet
of our old compromises. I stopped
to smell the roses, but the water was overflowing.

VI.

This is the vision that passed before the spectator.
Want doesn't equal hate.
& Love never equaled anything.
It would have been easy to complicate us
with projected verse, but I am the washing
away instead. I tried to be the panorama, that thing
that bridges all colors, that whispers to me
of *completion*. I wanted the landscapes we've

crossed to be a symbol we could hold onto
as the wetness seeped inside. I only needed a
black & white memory that meant *us*
to sustain the faltering of my steps
on this sodden landscape. What you needed was
a living hand, one that could reach out to you from
old Polaroids, one that sought to hold us both up.

From the Confessional

For me, it is hard to separate the self-elegy from the confessional, for I tend to conflate the two in my own work. In other words, much of my poetry circles around my own lamentations about the discarded moments, the forgotten fantasies, the missed opportunities, the poor life choices, and/or my past struggles with my interpersonal relationships with family, friends, jobs, work, etc. Almost compulsively do I dig internally, as if I am unable to shake the inherent narcissism that haunts all of us to some degree. To the outside observer (reader), this can be tiring to read at times, so I attempt to push the images themselves, make myself the inhabitant of the image, to hone in on the point that we are all influenced by the external, but can only process things internally. Hence, the act of introspection itself needs to be interrogated. The confessional poet is the one who does this almost out of instinct, habit, or compulsion. The self-elegist makes this interrogation a tool towards self-awareness, towards personal enlightenment, and in my own case, an acknowledgement that I am flawed, but searching for the truths behind my mistakes.

I think of how philosophers used to tackle this issue: Descartes's "Dualism," or attempt at proving a self "outside" of the mere flesh, as if we could ever be so sure of a Soul; or Emerson's "Eye"/"I" as an abstract, disembodied watcher of Truth. These sorts of mental searches for meaning/purpose/worth, all well-intentioned, tend to follow the same curve towards disappointment precisely because what they seek is too subjective to capture. This existential let-down is the core of my own poetic drive, and also perhaps why most of my poems tend to dance with the self-elegy style. It is as if I am in constant reflection and am more interested in what I "missed" or "misused" than what I achieved; a sort of perpetual mourning for the intangible possibilities of my own life's path.

Try It Yourself(ie): Poetics of Evidence/Persona

This exercise is linked to a specific author's poem (Mark Levine's "Work Song"), but can easily be modified to fit other work(s). In essence, it's a means to get to the self from the outside, through objects to be sure, but also histories and interpretations of those moments.

We all leave traces or "evidences" of our lives. What is our relationship to these things? What do they say about us, about you, about the "I" that is you? Can you conflate yourself with these evidences? *Have you already, unaware?* Think on your attachments to such objects as your car, your phone, your computer, your needs, your histories, the trails you leave behind as you move forward through your landscapes.

Look at yourself as "persona," from the outside. Abstract yourself from yourself as much as possible. Fabricate another you, one that you know, *but is elusive.* Find a way to interact with this other "you." Use devices and objects and image systems as you see fit but remember there are always many keys to unlocking various doors to yourself, this other self. Play the game, be relentless, hide nothing, point your fingers at *yourselfs.* Attempt to hide from yourself—see if you can. What gives you away? Your own self-mockery? Your irony? Your inability to escape from guilt or perceived obligations? Your Debts?

To complicate this even further, do not let yourself use similes—you are required to inhabit this poem. Be audacious, take a risk, conflate you and you and it and the thing. If it helps, think of many of the lines from "Work Song": "I am a zipper. A paper cut," or "I am a ticker-tape parade, I am an astronaut," or "I am scraps of / bleached parchment," or "I am an ice machine. / I am an alp."

Osteochondroma Lineage

1.

Elvis, hunk-a-hunk of burning love, plays over the speakers,
& you know such heat, to flush deep.

Spiraling in lines stepping up towards the Cliffhanger
at Six Flags Over Texas, you're naked in your bikini,

in the eyes & ankles of boys. A girl on the milk carton.
You'd flash breast to distract, trade one lump for two others.

Turn back if you could, step down
from rollercoaster bliss, shrieks of other boys & girls

who wait & stare. If bone could drip like wax, you'd incise
& blow gently to cool the cut. Let it bubble & build a way

beyond the skin, billow out, then be flattened, be smoothed
by the wind, so much harder here, a towering inferno over Texas.

2.

At a hotel bar in the Luxor Casino, you meet your second prostitute.
You, Julia & Melanie let yourselves be defined

by married men buying you drinks. Your first,
you danced together at a cantina in Ghana, scared brittle.

A girl of twenty, you envied her ease & sway
& perhaps she envied you. But when she touched your cheek

you walked away. You should've said you'd let her take it:
the calcium that in others builds, in you, kills,

let her surgery you, outline you on the ceiling & cut.
Blind body switch?

After cutting, you wait to touch because to feel the sawed-off limbs
means to love what you dream of leaving

& who falls in love with leaving?

3.
The one in Vegas knew better than to stand too close to you.
Could you steal her body too? She knew that desire spreads out
like any other wet thing, any exchange of fluids.

4.
But Las Vegas betrays the world's spinning axis, makes us believe
in time warps & warp speeds, that nothing in between.

Others taught you stillness:
The Musée Rodin beneath Orpheus,

who doesn't know he'll lose Eurydice again,
& Eve who cannot feel the cherry blossoms, wrapping her arms

like a noose in grief, like the female body & how it is played on.
La Saint Chapelle, colors to clothe yourself in.

5.
Every location is sterile until you leave behind chucks
of calcium & blood. Your mother,

like mountains, as if Rodin sculpted her arms & legs
& left the rest of her as human as possible, to sit & compress.

Outside, the mountains & desert of New Mexico compete.
They want to exchange scar stories.

You hear one ask another, shark bite? & you wish it were that simple,
something taken away but your story is added on.

With *missing*, you can create your own definitions.
But when a thing is present it is what grows in others' eyes.

Simply put, your bones are benign tumor growths.
You can lie & say, broken bones

or metal balls to stabilize, but denial is a betrayal—
As her bridesmaid, your friend Shannon requires black

tea-length dresses & red shoes,
high-heeled bullseyes. & it's worse, when no one asks at all,

& you're suspended in waiting.
Is vacancy the only true release?

Do we let go every time we gaze up at a neon sign?
To scoop the calcium out would be an advertisement.

6.
Billboard space for lease in holes & cups of bone.
Can a baby sign a lease?

When he said the condom broke, you thought he kicked
you from the inside, but there's still a little cup.

When you graduated college for the first time,
your mother gave you a white topaz ring, gold band.

Your grandmother died the second time.
For your third, your mother gave you a cameo necklace,

wanted to buy you a cameo bracelet as well but you're still learning
how to fold along origami lines, to river, to stand within

the one body, that gold frame & pale face, a smashed curio cabinet delight.

Self-Portrait with Framing Effect

—after Frida Kahlo's *"The Broken Column"*

is delinquent, an inamorata butcher,
cracked fang of things collected:

diamond cut vignettes
panoramic Venus hips
chase soundtracks.

Like potassium or plums
our bones produce, contract, read—

Sitting behind a screen
underneath blankets of leopards
& running stitches,

I almost forget I am a frame job:
how I sponge-curl my hair
or knife an apple.

Swirl
my 2 umbrellas, the one above
my drink & the one in my head.

How just wanting to locket
my excess calcium says I believe
DNA maps unequally even as

I try through leather straps & steel pins
to mash these given limbs together

I would say *again* but the idea that I was ever
whole is like a fable my mother told
when I couldn't sleep:

flags,
my flush face in the crowd,
twin smokestacks.

It took less than a crash to take me apart,
but Greyhound is what I remember.
All those dead babies & smooth limbs I couldn't feel
that might have been my own.

Advice to My Twenty-Four-Year-Old Self

I would say, *you worry about the wrong things*—

falling into routine as if into a salt pit,
rising as quickly as tar

never realize crooked bones don't make you sink
less   or   more.

I would say, *don't worry about the small things*—
be a monster   for a little while longer.

I would want to say,   *debt isn't invisible*—
the aftermath like freckles or swimsuit lines

if you never left your own head,
you still beach-waltzed the night in the arms
of an army guy.

I would try to show you,   *debt can be invisible*—
a shelter for homelessness

in secondary trauma locked doors & windows
can't guarantee safety

sometimes giving in feels like gambling.

[...] like the Log Run at Six Flags, assembly lines
of prepackaged chips & Barbies, you'll be
the girl never stepping out
of bounds. But you should know,

you can reframe   make your own
          velvet rope   & warning tape

[for & against] Wisdom

I am failing everyone who loves me, especially the ones
with tumors. I'm failing the way cowards fail—
running away & wishing.
I'm failing the natural order
by adding sugar to blackberries & salt to tomatoes,
by not becoming my mother.
I am failing late night calls of pain
& matching blue spider veins. *You don't know,* my mother says,
but I do—we do it to ourselves, can't unlace
like petals, so we close in, steal water
from stem until dying weaves into living—all lace.
& what is the body but a swimming pool
for the drowned & drowning neural vines of memory?
I am failing implicit & explicit memory.
I'm failing metaphor.
I'm failing my grandmother & her wish that I stay
"just the same," a "good girl."
I am failing the sky
& everything that falls from it.
I am failing wisteria & belladonna, rattlers
& garden snakes. I am failing girl & woman, student & teacher.
I will fail erasure since there are some places,
some people we will never be anonymous to.
I will fail like the words "Kara was here" smeared
on dirty windshields, like a car in a car wash fails its past.
I will fail my shadow & stillness. & when I move on
I will fail movement. I will fail to know when *enough is enough.*
I will fail this ending, this white flag, this tilled earth,
& the next.

Thirteen Ways to Self(ie)-Elegy

From moment to moment, I imagine new timelines, new futures drawn and erased, appearing and disappearing like wind. Like the sliding door effect. Like Schrödinger's cat. *What if, what could have been, what might have happened, what might be. . . .* For me, the self-elegy is a conversation between the self and possibility, introspection and hindsight. Not a therapy session (we can never be completely objective about ourselves) but a questing, a way to seek deeper empathy for the self and others. I can't help wondering who I would have been if I had learned not to be ashamed of my body. What if I wore bikinis and disability with pride? What if I hadn't learned to pose, to frame, to hide? So, while editing this anthology, I decided to create my own how-to self(ie)-elegy guide:

1. *Tilt Something*
Twist sideways, slant up or down. Angle the lens. Examine every direction: the before, the after, the in-the-moment, the in-betweens, the adjacent.

2. *Eyes Matter*
Look at the lens that captures you, not just the camera or hand holding it. Face what fills the cracks. What filters you choose.

3. *Lighting Matters*
Map fluorescents, regrets, and harsh judgements. The softness of sunrises, new beginnings and second chances.

4. *Know Your Shadows*
Cast the sun at your back to illuminate your silhouette.

5. Smile Normal
Don't fake what you don't feel. Be honest, flawed, and real. You didn't feel like writing a poem today, but you will try again tomorrow.

6. Pump Up the Background
Look at the context that defines you. Sunset, Rosetta Stone, protest sign, Frida Kahlo painting.

7. Seek Out Exposure
Share your failed experiments. Your failed words and failed poems. Failed dreams. The wisdom gained. What makes you ashamed.

8. Make a Flash Decision
Decide what moments to highlight, illuminate. Decide what seconds need more light or less.

9. Buy a Selfie Stick
To achieve a wider angle. Ask yourself, what creates distance? Time, a different point of view, reflection?

10. Get Inspired
Don't settle for the status quo. What gets you by. Look for the new, the different. Question what you think you know.

11. Try Portrait Mode
Let the background fade away, be the focus, reflect on what is going on inside you. And how it shows.

12. Practice
Look into the past captured in memory again and again. Even the same moment always changes. Try different angles. Remember, tilt.

13. Look for the Universal through the Personal

To explain self-elegy to myself, I turned to craft. My poem "Osteochondroma Lineage" was the first time I wrote directly about disability. Only through reimagining painful experiences—being exposed in a bathing suit while standing in line for a carnival ride or falling in love with superficial, commercial-ready moments—did I realize how much the world's perceptions of disability shaped me. How I often dreamt of waking into a new body, of switching roles, how I defined stillness as exposure. I would call this poem self(ie)-elegy for a few reasons. One, I think the poem is partially an attempt to explain that girl, the young woman I was, but also to say goodbye to her. I was trying to learn how to live within the body I was given. *To not be afraid to live in the body I was given.* Two, it speaks to absence; how, like our dead, when something's gone—erased, hidden, or in the past—you can define it anyway you want. You fill in your own gaps, create your own narrative. As far as goodbyes go, this poem failed. I failed to say goodbye to the girl I was—she's still here. But I have more empathy for who that girl was, and I began reframing my own self-creation myth. This poem is an artifact, as vibrant as any photograph, of who I was, and how a woman came to be. By understanding the past's influence on the presence, I can frame my own narrative without hiding. And who isn't tired of hiding?

Try It Yourself(ie)

Advice to a Former Self

Look back five or ten years. fifteen years. Twenty. What do you wish you had known back then? What advice would you give that younger version of yourself. What have you learned about beauty, truth, family, love, disappointment? Pick one to ruminate on. Or look to the future: what do you want the you ten years from now to know? Twenty years from now? What do you want to learn, to believe in, to accomplish?

For your poem, use the first person and directly speak to your other self. Try to use the conditional *would* and repeat the phrase "I would tell her/him/them" throughout the poem.

Choose one abstract concept such as beauty, love, disappointment to meditate on and use to frame the poem. To build imagery, add in specific, tangible images such as "warning tape" and "velvet rope" as a way to define your own way, your personal space. Consider adding in a contradiction about what you've learned, like how debt can be invisible as well as visible. Title the poem "Advice to My [INSERT AGE] Self."

Wisdom/Failure Poem

How can you show pride in your imperfectness? How can you find the beauty in your failures? Start listing your guilt, regret, disappointments, and triumphs through the lens of failure. What are you ashamed of? And see what gets exposed. How have you failed as a writer or at the other roles you've taken on so far.

For your poem, use the first person and include all the tenses of failure (to fail, will fail, failed, have failed). Remember to use descriptions at the micro level (grass, ants, atoms) and the macro level (constellations, cities, oceans). Be sure to use honorific language to praise and celebrate rather than pejorative language to criticize. Once you start writing, keep listing, past the point you think you should stop.

Self-Portrait with Framing Effect

Think of yourself as a selfie. Selfies are always framed: close up, angled, posed, filtered, touched-up. And meant to be shared. Think of the self-elegy as a selfie stick that allows you a little distance from the camera lens. With this distance, you capture a little more of yourself and your surroundings. So, pick a lens—girldom or parenthood, teacher or divorcée—through which to describe or frame yourself. Then pick a background that frames you, that informs the readers about you in relation to your lens. How do you see yourself? How do you want the world to see you? Is there a disconnect between how you see yourself and how the world sees you? If so, explore that disconnect to create tension in your poem.

Self-Portrait with Cable News, Graffiti, Weather

When I see the woman on TV, so calm
in her porcelain-white suit, I remember
that I too smiled while a man talked over,
that I bore the persistent tar of his voice.
In those meetings, I watched the veins
in his face like cracks in a disappointed street.
Were it not for his cruelty, I might have said,
I'm sorry for your loss. Who knows.
That year, my husband would overhear me
talking in my sleep, and though he couldn't open
the shut door of dreaming, he told me that I said,
fuck you, into the dark. Quite clearly, *fuck you.*
Night and waking were locked rooms,
the only exit a stuck window,
and the heat was always going or the cold.
Next order of business, a colleague said.
I noted every conversation—on the page,
no one interrupted. Often, remembering that year,
I hold a serving bowl, touch its surface
limned with flowers, this thing
I've dropped or knocked against a shelf,
the way it refuses, decorative, to break.
Now I can say *fuck you* quite clearly to that year,
although there was also the kindness
of friends who brought over cherries—
they knew I loved the sweetness of a stone.
I can say *fuck you.* I will not lose the taste for it.
In that year, I was, truth be told, willing to punch
a fist through glass if it meant escape.
I walked down Greenwood Avenue, past
the house where someone had sprayed FUCK YOU

on the road and someone else had tried
to X it out, pale lines on top of lines.
I understood wanting to write one's fury on a place.
I understood even the impulse to erase it,
walking each day across that imperative,
how it disturbed the concrete silence.
Most of us are not the woman on TV
who keeps talking, while the man is shouting
wrong into a mic—she keeps talking while
he stands beside her like a mugger in an alleyway
and who knows what he wants to take.
Most of us are the audience watching the debate—
we comply when the moderator says *no applause,*
no interruptions please. Most of us wait for night
to write FUCK YOU on a clean patch of asphalt.
All of this to say I could have said much more.
I could have written something on the man's sad face.
I think of him. I think of Greenwood Avenue,
its unremarkable houses that I learned to hate—
always moving towards a meeting or coming late from one.
I think of the sound that spray paint makes,
the rattle-shake of the can, the aerosol's soft hiss,
the words emerging slowly on a path, jagged perhaps,
but large enough, remaining legible through rain.

Through Rain

I wrote the first drafts of "Self-Portrait with Cable News, Graffiti, Weather" in the days after the 2016 election. I had spent that election season thinking about the discourse surrounding women—the ambitions women are permitted, how they are expected to express emotion, what it means for a woman to smile or frown—and about the recent upheavals in my own life. Only a few months before, I had moved halfway across the country, upending my life in order to escape a work environment so hostile and toxic that I thought it might kill me. My poems have always explored the tension between large-scale histories and small, intimate experiences. Therefore, it's no surprise that I saw in the events of the 2016 election season a mirror of my own, recent contact with misogyny and bullying. "Self-Portrait with Cable News, Graffiti, Weather" is a poem filled with anger, an elegy both for the optimism I felt in the lead-up to the election and for my former life. *Fuck you,* I write over and over again in the poem, voicing an anger that I wasn't previously allowed to articulate. The poem resists efforts to be silenced: the numbing bureaucracy of meetings, the men who menace and interrupt. It ends with rain attempting to wash away words on a pavement. But, the words stay, refusing to disappear. *Fuck you,* it continues to say. Whatever self was left behind—after the election results were announced, after the old life was abandoned—the poem asserts that it's enough for us to endure beyond the grief and into fury, "jagged perhaps, / but large enough, remaining legible through rain."

Try It Yourself(ie):
Self-Portrait with Cable News, Graffiti, Weather

Juxtapose a traumatic personal experience against an upsetting moment from the national news. Make sure the current event echoes, parallels, or illuminates the event from your own life.

For your poem:
- speak in present tense when writing about the current event
- speak in past tense when writing about your trauma
- move between these two tenses so that the reader begins to see how the intimacy of the personal and the public nature of a national event intersect
- be sure to use concrete detail and the five senses equally in both narratives—you want the private and the public to feel equally immediate
- end with an image that speaks to both stories

Minotaur

What stalked the room was never envy.
Is not regret, anymore,
nor fail. We are
—discovered:
we resemble hardly
ever those birds now, noising but
not showing from their double
cloisters—
leaves,
fog.
I miss them.
I forget what I wanted to
mean to you.
            I forget what I
meant to give to you, that I haven't.
Ménage.
You, in sleep still,
the dog restless, wanting
out, like a dream of the body caught
shining inside a struggling whose
end it cannot know will be
no good one.
Outside, the basil shoots to flower; the neighbors'
burro, loose, astray, has
found the flowers, his
head enters and tilts
up from the angle confusable with
sorrow,
adoration. His hooves pass
—like God doing, for now,
no damage to them—

the heirloom tomatoes: Beam's Yellow Pear,
Russian Black,
Golden Sunray, what sweetness once
looked like, how it tasted
commonly.
All that time.
I have held faces lovelier—lovelier, or
as fair.
        They make sense
eventually. Your own begins to:
fervor of a man
cornered; unuseful tenderness with which,
to the wound it won't survive, the animal
puts its tongue.

The Smell of Hay

If I speak of suffering.
I don't mean, this time, how it refines us,
I mean less its music than what is music-like
about it—a tendency to diminish to almost nothing, then
it swells back. The way memory can resemble steeple bells,
the play of them, the bell ropes having left
our hands. Or like snow resettling
inside a snow globe picked up, shaken,
set down. Then we shake it again. Lost excellence
is a different thing. Men who make

no exceptions. Men, who, because they expect everywhere
hard surprises, have themselves grown hard—fazeable,
fazed by nothing. Touch, as a form of collision;
a belief in divinity as a form of nostalgia. Husk of a libretto
for the world as—I can say it now—I wanted it: a room
that swayed with rough courtship; my body not mine,
any more to ransom than to refuse. On the window's
glass where the larger moths had beaten
against it, a find powder, a proof by morning I had only
to blow across. And it flew. It scattered.

Memory's Permanent Counterpart

I suppose I have a skeptical relationship to the idea of self-elegy, or maybe just an old-fashioned way of defining elegy.... For me, an elegy is a poem written with someone or something dead in mind. The elegy serves as a container for memory, is, in that sense, a more permanent counterpart to memory's tendency to shift unpredictably, if not entirely disappear or get reconfigured to a version of truth we're more comfortable with than with the actual truth.

Is a photograph of one's younger self elegiac? I don't think so, since we carry all of our younger selves inside us—I may not resemble myself as a twenty-five-year-old in a photograph now that I'm almost sixty, but when I look at the photograph I resonate with it, that earlier self comes more to the fore, inside me; it can do that, because it's still alive, because I'm still alive.

Likewise, then, if I say—as I do, in my poem "Minotaur"—that I miss what I used to resemble, or that "I forget what I wanted to / mean to you," can these be instances of elegy? If I've forgotten something, is it dead, or just not remembered? I do see "Minotaur" as an elegy, but not for myself—rather, for a dead relationship, or, more exactly, for a relationship whose death is imminent.

"The Smell of Hay" is a different matter. I suppose what I'm getting at in that poem is that excellence, once lost, can lead to an indifference to tenderness—which could be translated into an addiction to brutality, even when turned upon the self. It is an addiction that displaces excellence as easily as the speaker gets rid of the powdered remains of moths, something "I had only / to blow across. And it flew. It scattered." Is this an elegy for lost excellence, then? Or a shield to be brandished in the name of "rough courtship?" Hard to say, but not an elegy for the self; more a recognition that the self has changed, and the changed self brooks no regret.

Try It Yourself(ie): Translating a Taste or Smell

Pick a taste or a smell from memory and write a poem that never mentions that taste or smell. Instead, let your poem become a translation of that smell or taste, and of everything it brings back to you. The poem should be in two stanzas of equal length and should include a mix of complete sentences and fragments.

Refugee

Self-portraits of the new dark age are lonely
for the hand that holds the camera, the one

we never see. It is out there. On another
body, the one we live in, the one that floats

an ache here, an eyelash there, our fingers
drawn out of their hinges. Over the keys.

I am coming for you, hand, wherever you are,
whatever you suffer, you in the margins

of the movie that says we must be moving,
if not moved. Was it you who claimed,

the face in the light of the liquid crystal
waits only for the blackout to emerge.

I am holding out this camera for you, hand:
this plunder, this gift, the kind you give back

the way a wave gives back to the shoreline
or a small night boat to the open sea.

You will know me by the light of my study.
Take this shot, love. No, farther. Farther.

Language of the Refugee

The most social spaces are, too often, the most lonely, particularly if we are seen as someone we are not. Indeed, all personae are provisional, and yet, knowing this, we become more aware of who "we" (in a more elusive sense) remain. Sadly, we live in a culture of great loneliness, aggression, and verbal confusion regarding the "self," and the notion of the "self-elegy" invites an increasingly fraught and politically charged exploration of what it is we mean with the words that bind and divide us.

On the one hand, a theory-savvy culture, championed by such conceptualists as Vanessa Place and Kenneth Goldsmith, argues for the radical contingency and provisional, relational status of "selfhood," a notion suggestive of "identity"; but absent from their manifestoes are both a deeper psychological insight into the role that identity plays in all human development and the fact that such identity can never align with the "self" as the fundamentally unrepresentable field of subjectivity by which personae (as either publicly or privately performed) emerge as relatively phony or not. The two notions of self—as a construct and as that which defies construction—rarely find their distinction clarified in contemporary discourse, and yet both personal and cultural understanding depend upon it, as does a more penetrating examination into identity-driven patterns of cruelty and ignorance, both small and large. As Vanessa Place states in an interview with Jacob Bromberg:

> As I've argued before, and will again, in the age of semio-capitalism, where what we trade are signs and signifiers, most precious of which is the fungible unit of the individual—to wit, Facebook, Tumblr, mutatis mutandis—the poetic 'I' is the gold standard, the essential unit of exchange. Put another way, poets are the unacknowledged hedge fund managers of the world. Poetry pays." (White Review 2014)

For Place, the poetic "I" is thus a mere token of exchange, and indeed, if we discount the notion of the self as the unrepresentable and mercurial realm of the human subject, then that exchange takes on an exclusively relativized value. There is no "there" there, in terms of what constructs of identity strive (and fail) to model.

A social space, such as Facebook, articulates not only a genuine platform of connection but also a place to perform personae and affirm, with the compulsive inadequacy of the narcissist, one's identity as a vessel of admiration and envy. As with any compulsion, the imagined solution becomes part of the problem. The extremities of faith in the self as performed lead to greater alienation from the self as unperformable. The self-portrait figures as an elegy to or distancing from a more authentic regard for the self as unrepresentable. In "Refugee," the unseen hand figures as the real and (from the selfie's point of view) missing, living presence that made the portrait possible, similar to the unthought thinker in Husserl. The language for this self is darkness. Its boundaries are oceanic. Its space is social and solitary and more so the more insistently it calls.

Try It Yourself(ie): The Stranger in the Photograph

Write a poem addressed to the self in a photograph as if that self were another person. Try to forget what you think you know about yourself or the context; look at what the photo, and the photo alone, shows about this you that is not you anymore.

Vanessa Place, "Interview with Vanessa Place." Interview by Jacob Bromberg, Thewhitereview.org. *The White Review*, October. 2014, Web. https://www .thewhitereview.org/interviews/interview-with-vanessa-place/

A Body of Work

One comes, eventually, to the realization
that one will leave behind only
a body of work that will grow increasingly
unintelligible to each new generation. A trace
will remain spread across the vast
internet in much the way certain particles
inhabit the emptiness of deep space—negligibly,
though perhaps measurably. I, for instance,
am childless and, therefore, most likely
will die alone, my nest feathered
with yellowing poems. One comes, eventually,
to the knowledge that one's children
are increasingly unintelligible, being yellowing
poems spread across the emptiness of deep space—
negligible, though they once seemed, in their way,
to breathe. For instance, I am alive, right here,
in the middle of my poem, having had, perhaps,
too much to drink. One comes, eventually,
to the certainty that one's body of work
is nothing like another man's progeny, being
made of language which can only veer
toward emptiness as years become empty space.
For instance, hello? I am calling out to you,
folded here between the pages
of generations. You don't know me, but once
I was particulate and alive. Now what am I?

Giving It Back

An abandoned child by the gas pumps who said nothing,
a child who stared down the highway into the sun.

My life, which I have to give back.

Didn't see who left her, the station owner told the very young cop

while they walked her into the convenience store
and she ran her fingers over the brilliant candy rows.

My life, which I'm supposed to give back.

The cop unfolded his cell phone and
what kind of people would just drive off like that? the station owner said.

Such a pretty child, such a breath —
and my life, which I will have to give back,

which I'm supposed to return to You —

+

Everybody gives it back, Augustus blue-lipped in bed,
an unusual chill that summer, endless light rain,

or the hard winter of Aachen and Charlemagne at his window
admiring the snow, he'd felt so good that morning,

but now the fever returned.

Julian speared by his troops in the blinding sun.
Strychnine-veined, sweat-addled in his tent, Alexander among
    Chaldeans —

I could have given mine back under the fluorescent lights
where I came to buy cigarettes,

where that little blond-haired girl
has been growing wings this entire poem—

+

My father gave it back in Cleveland while snow
buried every car beneath the hospital window.

I watched the nurses grow winged,
watched them hover whitely above his body.

We must return what we have taken,
we must give back what we received,

and when he exhaled at last—
like an animal, low and guttural—

the nurses fluttered at the window,
they took his breath into the snow.

+

Thus, even my father returned what had been lent him—

and that little girl grows more beautiful
as she recedes into memory—

how they set her on the counter,
and she never said a word.

How I stood beside the magazine rack, five dollars in my hand,
and watched her flex those blinding wings,

how an hour later they would find the note in her pocket,

and would learn the way her father gave his life back
two miles up the road by the lumber yard,

site of personal despair, site of his return.

That little girl rose quietly into the air,
and her wings obscured the ceiling, they canceled out the lights.

I must give it back, I must return it to You,
I cannot hold onto this life forever.

Churches

In 1981
        in a hotel gift shop outside Phoenix, AZ,
a little girl stood by the postcard rack, turning it gently.
It creaked.
          She considered a picture of the desert, then
looked around for her mother,
                  who was elsewhere.
She gave the rack a firm push so it spun
gently on its axle,
          smiled, pushed it again,
and the postcard rack wobbled on spindly legs.

And soon she had it spinning
             so quickly the cards
made long blurry streaks in their rotation, gasps of blue
for sky,
      yellow for sand, and then faster,
the girl slapping at it with her hand,
                grinning at me,
and then a single postcard rose from the rack, spun in the air
and landed at my feet,
           a picture of a yawning canyon,
and then another, handfuls of postcards
rising from the rack,
         turning in the air
while the girl laughed
           and her oblivious mother, at the other end
of the store, bought a map or a box of fudge,
and then the air was full of pictures
             all of them shouting
Phoenix, Phoenix, Phoenix,
           twirling and falling
until the empty postcard rack
groaned once more, tipped,
and crashed through the window.

+

There ought to be a word
       that suggests
how we're balanced at the very tip of history
and behind us
      everything speeds irretrievably away.

"It's called *impermanence*,"
       the little girl said,
looking at the mess of postcards on the floor.
"It's called *transience*," she said,
       gently touching the broken window.
"It's called *dying*," she said.
     It was 1981
and the clerk ran from behind the counter,
       stood before us.
The girl smiled sweetly.
The postcard rack glittered
      in the sun and broken glass.
He turned to me and my face grew hot.
I couldn't help it. I was blushing.

+

In 2009, my father lay in a hospital bed
gesturing sweepingly with his hands.
       "What are you doing?"
I asked him. "I'm building a church," he said.
"You're making a church?" I said.
      "Can't you see?" he said.
He seemed to be patting something
in the air, sculpting something—a roof?—that floated above him.
The hospital room was quiet and white.
"What kind of church is it?" "I'm not finished."
"Is it a church you remember?"
      "Goddammit," he said. "Can't you see I'm busy?"

+

It was 1988 and I stood in line for my diploma
and my father took a picture
                    that I've lost now.
1984 and there we are
                    around a campfire I can't remember.
It was 2002
            and his cells began to divide wrongly, first one
deep in the wrist bone, then another
                        turned hot and strange,
deformed, humpbacked and fissured,
                    queer and off-kilter,
one after the other,
            though no one would know it for years.

+

"It's called *dying*," the girl said,
                        while the postcards suspended
in the air like a thousand days.
                I reached out to touch one,
then another,
            and all at once they fell to the floor.

Then the clerk said
                I was paying for the window,
where were my parents,
                and who was going to pay
if I didn't know where my parents were?
                        And the girl
smiled from behind the key chains
                    and her mother
pursed her lips at the far end of the store.
                        The window
had a hole in it through which a dry breeze came.
The postcards shifted on the floor.

+

Years later,
            my father was still making a church
with his hands.
            "They do that," the nurse said,
patting his head like he was a little boy.
                                    He was concentrating
on his church, though,
                        his hands shaping first what seemed to be
the apse, then fluttering gently down the transepts.
He sighed heavily, frustrated,
                        began again.
"Can I bring you anything else?" the nurse asked.
"No," I said. "Thanks."
                        "Are you sure?" She watched him
tile the roof, watched his finger shape another arch.
And then it was much later.
                        He'd fallen asleep.
Outside, snow covered up the cars.

+

"It's called *forgetting*," the girl said,
                            while the clerk
watched me and I blushed. "Until there's nothing left."
And a breeze entered
                    through the hole in the window.
"And then you're out of time," she said,
                            and shrugged.
Some of the cards were face up on the floor:
                                two burros
climbing a craggy slope,
                    the grand canyon like a mouth
carved in the earth, a night-lit tower like a needle.
                                    I was sweating now,
but I couldn't speak.
                    And then I was running from the shop,

past the fountain and the check-in desk,
down the tiled hall to the hotel pool,
where my father lay on a plastic beach chair,
                              reading a book about churches.
Sunlight flecked his chest.
                    His hair was wet from swimming.
"What's the trouble?" he asked.

+

First
    his cells were thick and soupy,
clotted and aghast.
                    Then they were spinning
through the air.
                    And it was 1986 and rain
drummed on the roof.
                    Or it was snowing, years later,
in Cleveland,
            his hands working the air
while the nurse stood in the doorway and sighed.
                              Wind and sun,
a bright day, a lovely day
                    to lie by the hotel pool and read
about how men spent lifetimes building them

and never saw them finished.

Immortality Lecture

There is a way to be both here and not here.

The cartoon cat stands just out of sight with the mallet.

The cartoon mouse peers from his hole into the living room.
Then yellow birds circle his head as he rises to heaven on angel's wings.

Your children have been watching TV for hours.

The cat peels the mouse from the floor,
drapes it over a piece of bread, and opens his mouth.

The sun butters the windowsill on a Saturday morning
in the summer before someone will die.

On the birthday cake, a single candle sputters like a fuse
the cat can't blow out.

The TV decorates their eyes with explosions of blue light.

Their heads are like little rooms
in which the mouse sits at his desk designing a rocket.

They will always remember you like this,
at your desk.

And so, the cat soars above the house and explodes.
Then the cat is in their heads designing a catapult.

I have implied that someone soon will die.

All morning, dead relatives
have marched through the room toward their rewards.

The mouse is drawing a door on the wall with chalk.
Now he is opening the door and stepping through it.

The cat has drawn a tunnel on the wall that flattens him.

Your children are bored. They've seen this one before
and are changing the channel.

You can never vanish from their world.

Interior Spaces

Before I can understand (for myself) what a self-elegy is, I need to understand the nature of the *self* in poetry. That is, I can't kill anything before I know what I'm hunting.

I believe, first of all, that writing poetry is a social act. That when a writer presents a poem to a reader, a social exchange has taken place—an exchange that in some ways resembles a thousand other social exchanges one makes every day. I am constantly presenting versions of myself to the world while, simultaneously, holding back many more versions. Every social decision I make—buying a sandwich, greeting a friend encountered accidentally on the street, writing or presenting a poem to the world—involves, on some level, deciding what to reveal, what to withhold, and how to present.

For decades, I refused to write directly about myself. I had an idea that the world of the *not-me* is far more interesting than the world of the *me*. That by limiting my subject matter to my own experiences, I crossed out possibilities for the infinite experiences of others and avoided a kind of narcissism I'd come to loathe in the works of my peers. Instead, I imagined writing a poem was something like disguising myself as someone else, then walking out into the world, whispering my invented story into the ears of my readers.

And that worked pretty well, this notion that the best place for the poet's self in the poem is deeply suppressed, if not nonexistent. I wrote poems I'm proud of, and assumed (to use the terms of this anthology) that any poem I should write would be a kind of self-elegy, in that I had killed off my "real" self in the act of producing the poem itself.

But, of course, this is wrong. First of all, to be able to deny that the act of writing poetry is an assertion of identity is naive. I'm a financially secure, straight, white man. Asserting my identity has almost always been safe and comfortable and never felt like a political act for which there could be consequences. It is easy for a person in my position to believe that poetry shouldn't be identity-based, but every poetic expression I make is an assertion of my own identity, no matter whose voice I'm using, what fictional tale I'm telling. The ideas, images, values, conclusions, opinions, stories, emerged from somewhere, didn't they? They emerged from the swamp of *self*.

I am very attracted to the idea that a poem might mimic the inner workings of a self—a mind—at work on vast and unsolvable problems. When a stanza ends, when a poet offers a moment of white space, he suggests a mind resting in unarticulated thought before the words arrive and the text continues. Free verse poems create performances of interior space and, for a moment, readers who experience these poems are like mind readers, listening in on the interior workings—the images, music, silence, thoughts—of another person. But that person—no matter how closely he resembles the poet, nor how far his lived experiences are from the poet's—is still, in some way, a version of how the poet understands minds to work and the world around him.

As such, the poet offers a version of a self, at the expense of all the other versions of the self that he does not offer. An identity is created out of many possible identities. A multitude of possible selves are erased in the service of the single self we experience in his poem.

This, to me, seems central to the idea of self-elegy: that in choosing a self to present, I had to erase all the other versions. All my poems that I selected for this anthology contain versions of myself and, of course, are expressions (even if inadvertent) of identity, background, class, etc. And, in some cases, certain things might be said to be "actually" true in these poems (whatever that means in art): I did meet a spooky little girl in a gift shop in Arizona when I was a boy, I did live near the gas station I describe in "Giving it Back," and I have often felt like the speaker of "Immortality Lecture." But that's not really the point.

To write the poems, I had to perform the act of erasing myself—of erasing many selves—knowing that true erasure isn't possible. And in that act, I was able to discover the poems and celebrate minds that exist in their difference from, and echoes of, my own mind. And that simultaneous erasure and embrace might be central to my understanding of the idea of self-elegy.

Try It Yourself(ie): Resonate Memory

Think of a memory that resonates for you. Perhaps it is a memory from childhood, a particular moment of fear or discovery. Perhaps it is more recent—a moment of complex bliss from last summer. Place yourself in the that memory, and then extend the memory in a direction the actual events did not take. Who might have been present (but wasn't)? What might have happened (but didn't)? Write that version of the memory—the version that didn't happen. Now ask yourself: If this version of the memory didn't actually happen to me, then whom might it have happened to? In other words, whose story am I telling? Who is this speaker? Is she different from me? She must be. Revise your writing to reflect the views, attitudes, and beliefs of the person whose memory your memory has become. Turn this into a poem.

Defining Self through the External

Even as we write and create, trying to exert agency and control, even as the term self-identity implies ownership, we shape ourselves based on other external forces. The self-elegy broadens the expected definition of relationship to include other external influences such as one's environment and community, not merely a lost loved one. When we define ourselves, and when we choose to define ourselves by other roles—as daughters and sons, wives and husbands, mothers and fathers, lovers and heartbreakers, teachers and poets—we acknowledge that, like the self, those external forces are temporary and always changing. Even in absence, perhaps especially in absence, the external other defines us to some degree. Can we choose to not be defined by external factors? By outside expectations? Or are these factors always tethered to us? Through hindsight and self-elegy, we explore the place this other still maintains in the world. In this way, perhaps the dead are never truly dead, and what is lost is never truly gone.

keep your face to yourself and remain blind

–after Cees Nooteboom

(1)
WE KNOW THAT GROUNDWATER SEEPAGE can occur

sometimes hours, sometimes

only minutes before an earthquake.

Any leak might be an opening of disaster's artery.

Each might be so narrow and colorless

that they require the looking eye's exquisite intuitions.

Outside my bedroom window, before dawn, I hear them.

The day-laborers are back, they've come

to work in the vacant lot across the street.

First, they're killing weeds, then they're sifting gravel from larger rocks,

then sifting sand from gravel.

I sift from my listening

the vigilance that is astute, not simply obsessive.

Vigilance will be useful to apply to the listening I'll do

throughout the day.

I'll keep my curtains closed to daylight.

I stitched them myself from a linen

of the quietest color

so that the least sound in my bedroom

would find in them a resonance that could make the dark respond

to the hue of every shadow cast by my breathing.

(2)

IN ORDER TO WARM my hands in bed on a cold evening

I often reach under my pajamas and hold my breasts.

The chill is uncomfortable at first, but I will myself to continue.

Then I feel how the sense of touch moves from volition, by increment,

to meet strangers who are hidden between more obvious sensations.

Outside my bedroom window, I watch one narrow

long-reaching branch replace the more obvious horizon.

(3)

MY EARLIEST bedroom had no window. Its wallpaper

was window enough, patterned

by my adoration of its stillness so pure

that it became the depth within me

that I could use my hands to seek

and sometimes find.

This morning I watch out my window

as a day-laborer outside takes off his work-gloves.

Some precisions must be sought bare-handed,

some precisions imbed,

with the rigor

of a thorn working its way in. Some are an incisor,

sharp with the need to appease a hunger

I needn't name, biting

through to a history unknown to me, an action

not to be confused with living.

(4)

I HOLD STILL until stillness

isn't an act of body but a conversation with my dead,

a portrait observable from only one side,

its pigment extracted from the past. Its paint

never dries.

(5)

DEAD, SHE IS NOT my mother, she is one side

of my coffee cup, the un-witnessed side. Though I move around

our conversation, around the table I've set for it, and I sit down

in each different chair,

there remains a side of this cup I can't see.

My left hand is again

cupped around my right breast,

as it often is when I'm thinking

of the past and the future

as sensation, as a discussion between

palm, nipple, and the occasional seismic

tremors that their touching will cause.

(6)

I go to museums when I can.

I wander the galleries

until I find a portrait that I choose by intuition.

I stand a little to the side, never catching the figure's eyes,

waiting until the brushstrokes that create the face

extend beyond my recognition of the frame.

Watching is a sensation

that extends in the way that my nipple extends

when I touch my breast with my hand.

what I thought I could lose . . . and what I thought I had lie next to each other

—after Mei-mei Berssenbrugge

(1)
THE OTHER OFFICE EMPLOYESS think my work

is easy for me. It's what I work

to make them think, and to make myself forget

how hard it is to work inside this small box.

Its dimensions are less than an arm's reach.

Inside the box, I sweat and I scab

worse each week.

(2)
BRUISES FROM THE HARD WALLS of a small box

can be negotiated

if I hold myself awake, hold my body sustained between

top, bottom, and all four sides.

The worker I am still has the unquestioning strength

of the young. The worker I am works hard to believe this.

(3)
MY WRISTS ARE WRENCHED BACK, then come right again,

my knees loosen then lock on demand,

my thighs press to raise my spine

against the top of the box as its ceiling shifts without warning

to become one of its sides, then its bottom, then its side again.

(4)
THERE IS NO MEANING but

the meaning of holding myself leveraged

on all sides. All that I need know

of myself as myself

is this constantly revising version of upright.

(5)
DAILY I DRAW punctuation marks on my work notepad.

I once believed in periods, but no matter how many

I drew, nothing ever stopped.

Now I've begun a series of apostrophes

that have released themselves

from the words they made possessive,

and become free-floating wings.

If they let me wear them, then I will be safe

in my small box

no matter how much it spins.

Archeology of the Present

When I imagined the meanings resonating for me in the idea of a self-elegy, Giorgio Agamben's view came to mind:

The entry point to [perceiving] the present necessarily takes the form of an archeology; an archeology that does not, however, regress to the historical past, but returns to that part within the present that we are absolutely incapable of living. For me, Agamben puts into words some of what I intuit about poems that I consider self-elegy. In them, I am seeking what is lost, what is past, what I had not seen when I lived that time, and what I might assume is dead to me, dead in me. Yet it is in seeking that death—those deaths of my self (selves)—that so many of my most challenging and valuable insights arise. The work is not logic driven; I write sensing my way in a dark that is not blind exactly, but that has been sense deprived.

I've read that we choose to disassociate rather than face a pain we cannot tolerate. Such disassociations serve us, keep us sane. Yet once the dangers have passed, it is a question without answer to ask: can I return to that past which I was incapable of living? No, and yes. Writing is a paradoxical enterprise, as one journeys into one's aporias.

There's more though, for me, to what Agamben says. His words help me remember something else I've read: we all are, all the time, unconsciously making choices to screen out some of the constant barrage of experience. This is necessary and healthy. If we didn't, we'd go mad with the all of *the all of it*.

But such choices are a result of what I've taught myself: what I will let myself sense, and what I let myself ignore. How much of what I'm screening might be useful?

So, even in any given moment, even right now, deaths are happening; possible awarenesses are being killed off. . . . This is true as I am engaged in writing a poem, and seems especially important to consider when writing a poem of self-elegy. So, when doing this work, I want to keep some part of my awareness open to the idea of inviting in intuitions of the deaths going on in every moment of the writing itself. Sometimes, in those moments of writing a poem, the experience of those deaths enters the work itself; it widens, it speaks up, and changes everything I thought I was doing!

As I wrote the two poems here in this collection, and then later as I reengaged with their first drafts (I call it radical revisioning), I experienced some glimpses of this. I see self-elegy as a way to write, not only about the past, but also to write in the moment, of the moment (letting my loose focus stay awake to the fact that so much is lost to perception in the moment of writing, so much that I have not allowed myself to see).

I see poets doing this work in poems of theirs that I love (it may be part of what I love in those poems), and I seek it in my own poems. In the act of writing, there's the chance to sense a little more into that death/those deaths (happening all the time), into those lost places, moment by moment, as they occur. In writing, there's the chance for me to have the courage, sometimes, to see what will surprise me.

Try It Yourself(ie): Archeology of the Present

A quote from Giorgio Agamben has been generative for me when beginning a poem, many of those poems are deeply aligned with the idea of self-elegy. I will paraphrase it for concision: A valuable way to come to better understand the present moment we are living (and use that understanding to write) is by archeology, but not an archeology that delves into one's known historical past. Instead, it is an archeology that mines the part of the past that we were actually incapable of seeing, and thus living.

For me, a poem of self-elegy begins as I realize that a part of me died during a painful, shocking, numbing experience in my past. I don't try to resurrect that dead self, instead I allow her energies to infect/infiltrate me in this moment. . . . Here is one process I use:

First, I choose randomly, I let any memory that surfaces by the source, and **free-write:**

- all the **objects** I see in the room or location in which it occurred
- all the **parts of my body** I can visualize, while in that body, as if they were objects in action; what are they doing?

- all the parts of **any other bodies** that I visualize, as if they were objects in action; what are they doing?

Second, I look around the location I'm in, in moment of writing, or a few hours before, and then do the same thing as in "a" but for the present. So I free-write:

- all the **objects** I see in the room or location
- all the **parts of my body** I can visualize, while in my body, as if they were objects in action; what are they doing?
- all the parts of **any other bodies** that I visualize, as if they were objects in action; what are they doing?
- free-write about **any news item** that strikes me [for instance, in one poem of mine, I started it by imagining that I was experiencing the groundwater seepage that someone reported seeing just before an earthquake . . . this somehow aligned for me with the shock of revelation that a disaster was about to strike me in my personal life . . .]

Third, I begin another page (on my laptop, in my notebook), and randomly choose some of the work of my free-writes from the past and from the present and say more about them.

I might collage some together. . . . I let myself be fearless and if I feel lost, I write about the feeling of lostness. . . .

A Whale-Like Singing

I will always live with the blue body,
blue baby who could barely breathe and I
bury him inside me, especially when I
sit across from my son in a restaurant
or diner—the kind of half-way point where
we tend to meet now that he has his own
newly adult life, and I find myself under
my breath chanting *live, breathe, live*
as if were I to stop the plane of his life
would spiral down into a plume of smoke,
as if only my attention keeps it in air.
The name for this is PTSD and no wonder
my son pulls away, eyes me with alarm,
the fear that rises from my palms,
and I want to say "It's okay, it's okay,
I screamed, and you began to breathe
though it took three exchange transfusions,
you came alive just as I always knew
you would." But that isn't the truer story.
The truer story as I remember was just
the being there. I had to buy shoes in
the hospital gift shop and all they had were
size six men's vinyl slippers, and they let
me sleep in the spare beds—an hour
here, an hour there—while I waited to see
what would happen: my blue child in
his blue incubator—my shoes squeaking
as I walked the late-night hospital halls
and that one time I went running into
the NICU, chasing a humming sound,

and it was him—he was like a whale, they
said, sounding so he would not be alone,
and I stared through the glass at his mouth
moving out and in.

Velvet and Pins

Is it the eight titanium pins
around my knees or the fact

that for three months

the incisions were left open? I grew

to know that plush of inside—
the velvets, the iodine to prevent infection,

the smooth of body cast
like another girl who was exactly

my shape, but calmer than I would ever be.

She lay still, barely shifting, like a vase holding a flower,

which was me with my hot dangers, my
itchy despairs.

In the myth, the girl who is Spring only gets her
power when she chooses the mask of bone.

I did not want the world to be this way.

For weeks, I stared at the dull view out the window
of alleys in moonlight, a few sunken garages,

a dirty-white cat. I stared until these things
became beautiful again.

Something closed inside me, which glinted
like a sharp bright pin.

Self as Last Call

To be like the swallows, building
nests of mud under the eaves of sagging houses.
To lay three eggs, hatch three chicks,
and watch one of them fail to thrive each time.
To be destined to fly further than a lifetime,
across a continent, three oceans, until you cannot
even picture the place you started from.
To walk in snow until it makes you feel
warmer, and you lie down to make an angel
the way you did at six, a little paralyzed
by the too-vivid image of a body pressed
on earth, hands raised as if fighting against
or straining toward.

Patriarchy

Today, you are the skin on the water.
You shiver and the waves shift—foam and detritus on the smile of the
    beach.
I hum and hum you.
Sometimes a song you once sung to me like the siren on the lonely rock.
Who are you, but an I my I can't erase?
I find a picture of you stuck in my drawer.
I blank you in parts with a Bic ballpoint.
The nib clicks against the paper like a rake against a dry field.
I picture blackbirds lifting in clouds,
angles of words I don't know how to feel.
Grammar, which is related to glamour,
the flimflam aspect of longing or loneliness.

Vivisection

How you bisected me—
the elegance of the scars.
The disease? It was not chemical.
you could not cure it.

I cling to this chill.
Watch how I unfurl
before it, flag of myself,
a mirror distorted. This body—

it is nothing. In an instant,
I could transform it.
Now it is a lake, spreading
outward; now small and blank,

a flat stone poised
in a hand. It breaks apart.
Only the grains of it.
Listen, how they drift and scratch.

The old shapes, the forms
that were broken, are still here.
They reassemble, a buzz,
a communion.

They promise me courage,
other virtues, the rough shield,
freedom from pain. They tell me
I am this or this—

tube of calcium, star
of blue phosphorus burning.
Now the reenactment:
Chips fall from a chisel,

joints burst into loud
red flower. A bird flies
out of my mouth
and into the ceiling.

On Why So Many Female Self-Elegies Are Melancholy

I am curious about how to remember my past selves here, now, I am curious because if a self-elegy is in part an audit, a self-audit—a kind of slow internal reckoning, in which you weigh who you were, where you were headed versus who you are, where you are going—then it is hard not to feel that for many women this process has become more complex, a revisioning, a revising in the most basic ways.

For example, I can't watch some movies or even most movies I used to love and/or find romantic. Recently, I caught a few minutes of "The Breakfast Club," which my teenage self once found "cool" or "sweet" in a fun cheap celluloid kind of way, but now as I watched it, all I could think about was the various multifaceted ways it reified all the imprisoning things girls were taught to do or think about themselves—and that scene where Judd Nelson feels up Molly Ringwald under the table—that scene makes me want to vomit or weep.

****

I used to say nothing like that ever happened to me and then I remembered.

****

Once, in eighth grade I was standing outside my junior high school, Alice Deal Junior High. I had just started smoking cigarettes, which I would get from my friends—Leslie and Vivian—and so I was standing on the corner of Nebraska Avenue at the bus stop smoking a Salem cigarette Leslie had given me which was a little crushed and even had a tear in it. I was wearing my favorite army pants and a halter top—it was May; I was almost in ninth grade—that had a pattern of sunflowers and cartoon-type turtles on it.

The car that pulled up was blue, that pale blue they used to paint cars before metallics became popular that was very flat and matte, like a child's idea of sky, and the man inside was about forty and wearing a striped suit. Later, I would think to myself that he had a faintly turtle-like face, by which I meant he looked a little like Roger Mudd, who was a famous newscaster back then, and, also, was said to be a distant relative of mine on my father's side. The Mudds of Missouri. This man in his seersucker suit looked like one of the Mudds, and his car was wide and expensive-looking.

He said, "Are you hitchhiking?" and I said "yes." It was not so unusual to hitchhike in those days, but I said yes, even though I wasn't, or wasn't intending to, and later I would be haunted over why. He said "You shouldn't be doing that. I know your father. He wouldn't like it," and because this strange man said he knew my father with such confidence, I believed him, and later, I was ashamed of that, too. He said he would give me a ride, and I could just get in, and so I did, and we drove a moment in the hum of air-conditioning, and then he put his hand on my thigh and he let his finger climb up to my crotch and he rubbed me there through my pants.

No one had ever done that to me before, and it was so unexpected, so utterly strange that I didn't do anything for quite some time or what felt like quite some time, and then I was afraid, and I noticed he had locked the doors of the car.

I said then, beginning to panic, I said, "Please let me out, I am going to catch the bus," and he—he had sandy hair, balding, combed-over, red-yellowish skin, freckles, he said nothing. He just kept his hand where it was, and I moved away, but not very effectively, and I tried to figure out how I would unlock the doors of his car without him stopping me—and then; what a strange thing, we were behind a bus, and there were a bunch of girls from my junior high school on it—Mikael who was in choir with me and Shantel, who was known to be bad because she smoked weed in the girls' bathroom, and they started waving and sticking their tongues out at me, and I said "I know them," and he pulled the car over to the curb and said "You can get out now." He did not look at me, and I got out of the car.

****

I didn't tell anyone. I never told anyone—not even Leslie or Vivian, who were supposed to be my friends. I didn't because I was ashamed I had gotten in the car; I felt vaguely guilty because I had not seen it coming, or because I had not stopped him loudly enough, or because my fear had somehow made me immobile, because I could not quite believe it, because I had believed this man—who seemed about my father's age—surely knew my father. Because

I was afraid he did know my father, as awful as that seemed, because when I thought about the whole thing I was afraid this was something he probably did to a lot of girls, and what if Mikael and Shantel had not been on the bus, and what if they had not started making faces at me?

****

That was one thing I had forgotten until I remembered it. Here is another. This happened years later. I was twenty-six or twenty-seven, and I was at the Mars Bar on the Lower East Side, and a German girl, who I knew only vaguely, and who was tall and glamorous—and because of this I felt some-how beholden to her—asked me if I could buy her some D, which was what we called heroin back then. And although I was a desultory druggie at best—a neophyte really—somehow, I agreed to walk with her down to the projects on Avenue D, where another guy at the bar told us you could go to this one building and buy your drugs.

I must have been drunk, more than a little, though not so drunk, I couldn't find my way. The German girl gave me the cash, then said she was too afraid, and would I do it for her, and I said "sure," which was how I wound up inside the building, heading up to the fourth or fifth floor.

The drill was you rang the buzzer on the door, a green door, at the end of the black-and-white-tiled hall and they opened the door, and you gave them your money, and they gave you the drugs and that was it, but that was not what happened to me.

When they opened the door, the guy on the other side pulled me inside. He was about my age, skinny, with a scraggly moustache and hands that trembled a little, and he said, "I know you are a cop; tell me you are a cop," which was ridiculous because to my mind I wasn't even tall enough to be a cop. And I was about to say this, when I noticed he was holding a gun. The gun looked light and small and almost toy-like, but it also looked real, the realest object I had ever seen.

I said I just wanted to give him my money, but my words garbled, and he said because I was so nervous, I must be a cop. And maybe because I was drunk, I didn't cry or scream, I just said "I don't know why you would think that," and he said I better come into the kitchen and he waved me forward with his gun. It was a pretty ordinary kitchen, except there were drugs on the table, a pile of tiny packages in the kind of semiclear, parchment-like paper they used, crudely stamped with little pictures and the brand name.

The table was formica—the kind that is beige with gold flecks, and the floor was linoleum and beige also, and it was curling up at the edges. The kitchen cabinets looked the same as the ones in my apartment, a little grimy around the edges, a couple open, empty, with roach motels perched in the corners.

He pointed the gun at my head. He told me to sit down in the chair. There were other people in the apartment. Young boys mostly. They were moving around in rooms I couldn't quite see. Sometimes the doorbell rang, and one of the boys would answer it. He said "tell me you are not a cop." And I thought for a moment I was going to die there, and so I began to speak.

I spoke like some crazed Scheherazade on speed. I told him I had been a child who loved the woods. I told him there was tree I climbed. I told him about the first cat I ever owned who died. He interrupted me a few times too, but what he spoke didn't make much sense to me. I realized at some point he was either so high he had lost himself or maybe he had not been to sleep for a very long time. He would ask my name, and I would tell him, and he would forget it, and so I would tell him another story instead.

I was conscious primarily of a desire to please and, in-between thinking I was going to die, I was worried about the German girl waiting for me at the corner of Avenue D and 7th Street.

Meanwhile I keep speaking. He put the gun down on the table between us. He stood up to get a glass of water. I was scared he would touch me; I was terrified he would touch me, but he didn't.

****

What were the stories I told him? As far as I can recall, they were mostly about places—houses I had lived in, or yards I had played in. I had lived in many countries, and this seemed to give me a peculiar advantage. At some point, he began to speak, too. He told me before he had come to New York, he had lived in an island. Everything he remembered about the island did not feel real to him.

He picked up the gun and said, "This is real," and I found myself nodding. I had a slight desire to hold the gun, but I knew I never would. I knew if I got out of there, the one thing I would be able to see in my mind forever was the gun. I would not be able to remember his face, but I would remember his hands, which were slim-fingered with short slightly ragged nails as if he bit them.

****

There was a moment, after hours or what felt like hours, when the light out-side the windows changed, paled and blued, and I said I should go, which was terrifying to say, and he said "Okay" and pushed a piece of paper towel toward me and said I should give him my number.

I wrote out the number in big block strokes with a blue Bic pen, which he also gave me, and I took care to make the last number wrong, and all the way down in the black elevator and the hallway with the tiny black-and-white tiles I felt guilty as if it had been a date, and I was blowing him off. When I got out in the street, I realized I still had the German girl's money, but I never saw her again.

****

Sometimes that winter my phone would ring and I would think it was the guy with gun and I would let it ring and ring until it stopped.

And this was the only way I could gauge how afraid I had been.

****

Elegy means: "a poem of serious reflection, typically a lament for the dead." Elegies by their very nature are melancholic—a symptom of sorrow or re-gret. A self-elegy would seem logically to be a lament or a mourning for a self that is past or gone; that is dead to the present self somehow, but when I think about the notion of "self-elegy" in relation to these two very particular stories, I keep thinking about how what I want to reflect upon, is the ways in which I appeared moving through them, dead to myself. I mean by that, of course, not a literal deadness, but the peculiar deadness or inertia that appears central to what one might call my role or function in these plots. I know why I didn't speak or speak loudly enough in that car. I know why I didn't tell anyone, and this not speaking, not telling, seems at once personal and impersonal the way air is impersonal, a condition of my being or my being then as a girl in the world.

Similarly, in the second story, when I remember my speaking—even though I truly cannot remember the details of what I said, I remember a familiar feeling within that speech, a mode of being. I mean I remember it as I remember speaking to my parents or my teachers or any authority figure: I was speaking to please; the only difference, really, was that in that particular case, I was also speaking in order to survive, and within that was a similar inertia or deadness—I was speaking for myself, but not of myself. I can remember little of what I said to the man with the gun, but I do know this: the comparison to Scheherazade is in no way merely metaphorical. I felt I was singing for my life, and the stories I was telling all had this one simple purpose—to keep him amused enough, distracted enough that he would not think to use the gun.

****

I am not sure why I think of self-elegy in some sense as an audit, a reflection, a cataloguing, a valuing, but I do. I am sure I am not alone in this, but in the post-#MeToo era, with so many stories pouring out that are familiar, though not exactly the same as these stories, which again are examples, but not the only stories of this type I could tell, I find myself revisioning who I have been in way that is certainly elegiac as in "mournful, melancholic, melancholy, plaintive, sorrowful, sad, lamenting and doleful," but is also simultaneously impatient with the very forms and practices the elegiac posture has historically offered us—and by us, I mean myself, I mean the girl I was, I mean women. I realize the self-elegy I most want to write is one that could somehow reenvision the posture I took, the position I found myself in, and this tension feels to me somehow valuable, if painful. Who might I have been had I had been more empowered to resist? What stories might I have told had I not been afraid?

Walter Benjamin once said that "Our deepest nostalgia is always for the potentialities of the present." I have always loved that quote, and I have always felt I understood it, without being able to quite explain precisely what he might have meant. Yet this seems to me precisely the paradox of the practice of self-elegy—to look back and honor and lament what one believes one is no longer. To do so nostalgically would merely be to enshrine the forms that have been, but for women now, for me now, trying to grapple with who I am here in 2018, when so many women are telling their stories and when power seems as weighted against us as ever, then perhaps to engage in the practice with an eye on the potentialities of the present is at once more troubling and more revolutionary.

Try It Yourself(ie): Scars and Skin

Scars and skin. Thinking about scars and skin—or about what your skin and its "damage" tell you about yourself—can be a great way to construct a poem. Think about what scars do or signify or how they change the skin that houses you. Tell the story of a particular scar or engage with the idea of a scar as a border or seam, something that traces a rupture and is simultaneously a point of contact, much as skin itself is the boundary between us and the outside world, us and other people but also the first point of contact. Some poems to look at: "Scar" by Emilia Phillips, "The Time Around Scars" by Michael Ondaatje, and "Body Language" by Kenny Fries.

The Bedroom is a Labyrinth I am Lost Inside

I need instructions on how to open again.

Like a woman made of expertly folded maps sewn together,
my husband's first wife appears on the edge of the labyrinth

with familiar advice: *Lie back and think of a rose garden.*

When she pantomimes the instruction, "lie back,"
her body makes a sound like an urgent man

ripping open a delicate envelope with his thumb. Inside her

is the most beautiful invitation—intact and on linen, her address in gold.
The curve of each letter loops back to its rightful owner.

If you so much as hesitate, she warns, *he'll come hunting for me.*

With ease, she slides through the glisten of a hedge
I didn't even know was parted. I hide

in the curved belly of an unnamed fountain, drained. Still,
my husband finds me, lifts me out, and cleans red algae

---

from my fingernails. Everyone has something to say about how to
get over it, but my husband, every time he touches me, is all thorns.

I Became a Mother Overnight

have you ever dropped / a diamond ring / down the open throat /
of a sink / a loss lodged / in some / impossible world / only heroes
can reach / you want to rip up the pipes / shake them out / like sea serpents /
surely it's / here / it was / just / so / near / your body / but now it sails /
away from you with your every curse / and the tide / won't mind /
like it used to / you grip the porcelain / stare into / that ring of gold /
and green / and rust / for what you were / trusted not to lose / you play
the what if game / but / you / don't / win // that's how my old life left

I Take a Break from Annotating Our Will and Drive Down to the Antique Store

When the ink won't dry fast enough.
When your spine won't behave against the wingback chair
because the ghost won't leave the pattern in the wood
alone. He counts your vertebrae with his middle finger.

When the store is open anyway. When its door
is the right amount of miles away
from the signature lines of my last testaments.

When the gnarled woman at the glass counter
is reliably bitter in her apron, which is ruined
by the wells that leak ink, but you love her
for making you feel light as the dust on her coins.

When your dress contains no dollars.
When your pockets are a hive
of clicking lipsticks you should have thrown away:
English Rose, The Emperor's Trigger.

When the path to the backroom isn't distracted
by mirrors. Or chandeliers with broken tapers.
Or conflicted beneficiaries. When it's too hot
for other customers to wander that far.

And the backroom still has that bed—the same model
in which your parents dreamt through your childhood.
And there's a price in handwriting other than your own.

The sun catches in the window, and you remember how,
as a girl alone on the rug below your parents' bed,
you'd ask yourself which of its two colors was your favorite.
The reliable, hushed olive or the wilder riot of ice blue?
You'd demand an answer—which shade you'd keep if you had to.

And because no one shuffles across the store's floorboards
to ask you if you see anything you like, you lift
your heavy bones into your parents' bed. You ache
for home, where the bitty frame of the girl

you were once hopscotches across
the carpet's burn, loving each hue, on the edge
of her decision. How easy it was then
to imagine a world with only one color.

My Husband Brings Home a Terrarium

His gift dared me to lift its lid.
When I did, the unlocked swamp
cast off its fever, a hot breath
metallic as the gold doorknobs

of Espiritu Santo Church,
so hot they could disappear
fingerprints if you lingered,
unsure about your own burning.

But then the scent shifted deeper,
a scene before Sunday mass
when one of the Dewberry boys
whose blonde hair shined

like the cloth across Christ's waxy hips
put his lips to my pierced ear
and whispered that I had a voice
like deep fried barbed wire.

I pulled my knees to my chest
and temper-kicked the hymnals
in front of me, stamping
my white patent leather shoes
into all those prayers bound
by the most desperate believers.

The dirt caked on my Mary Jane's
fell to the marble floor, settled
in the shade of that humid world
under a church pew in the South,

beneath the rust-scented sins
of local husbands and wives
who hide their secrets behind
cans of Aqua Net and razorblades.

Where is that dirt now?
And is it in fact like love
in that it can never disappear?

Outside of the Frame

O f the four self-elegies that I have the honor to share in this anthology, "I Became a Mother Overnight," is the most autobiographical. I usually hesitate to claim that my poetry is autobiographical, but this poem captures a sentiment that I did experience: a parent's nostalgic yearning for the ease of life before children. I lived alone for six years before I got married; after my wedding, my life changed dramatically. I suddenly dwelled in a brick house with a husband, stepson, and a border collie. I desperately wanted to be a good wife and stepmother, but it wasn't as simple as turning the dial on a washing machine to unlock a different mode. "I Became a Mother Overnight" captures the struggle I felt during that adjustment period—the surprise, self-doubt, confusion, and to an extent, the loss of identity.

And yet, this self-elegy offers an incomplete vision of my experience. There was also a wealth of rose-colored moments that I experienced as a new wife and mother which never make a cameo in the poem. "I Became a Stepmother Overnight" delivers a tonally frantic and mournful palette that is limited to the initial shock of my transition into motherhood. In that first year, I struggled, sure, but I also reveled in the richness of family life. There was a sense of belonging in the warm connection of my little tribe—two beings who cherished me as much as I cherished them. Before long, I found myself smiling as I crafted healthy afterschool snacks, folded my stepson's laundry, and tucked him into bed at night. I suppose the self-elegy camera can only capture so much in one shot. As of this writing, I have been married for ten years, so I feel relieved to no longer grieve with this speaker. Still, I value this piece because it serves as a snapshot of an earlier time in my life. A hallmark. A memento. All in all, I am grateful for the chance to reread the poem and celebrate how much I have grown as a parent.

Reflecting on this poem makes me wonder if a self-elegy must be autobiographical. Poetry does not have to announce its connection to the author's life in the way that prose does, so why would a poem labeled as "self-elegy" be held to a different expectation? My poems exist in this push-pull between personal experience and imagination. Most of my work is born out of an image from my personal life that quickly takes on a life of its own. Much like being a parent, I enjoy the experience of planting the seed of the poem and watching it blossom however it is going to blossom.

Try It Yourself(ie): Crossroads Between Personal Experience and Imagination

Must a self-elegy be autobiographical? Think of an idea or image or a moment from your personal life, but then twist and distort it with the use of surrealism until the poem takes on a life of its own. Let a drain become an "open throat," let pipes be shaken out "like serpents." Look to surrealist painters like Frida Kahlo, Dorothea Tanning, Marc Chagall, Renee Magritte, Vladimir Kush, Lenora Carrington. How can this imagery connect to your personal experience? Let the unexpected imagery of these painters influence the imagery in your poem.

How My Body Mourns

How my body mourns
what it might have been, should be:

supple as a vine, lovely as the satin moonflower,
how my body mourns;

how thin molecules, sharp, desiccated, swarm
my bones, stretch the planes of my face;

how ancient genes want out, how
a radical softness, a membrane

from the normal mucus of my vulva,
climbs along my thighs and back and breasts;

spreads rich and eager across my flesh
and lies along me like a finger trails a stream

and I move to a man's rhythm: his in and out,
his arms and breast and hair and tongue;

how my body longs for rest from itch, from its own
false, desert self.

Madame X

I want to be you, Madame X, famous Parisian beauty.
I want to walk in your satin skin, feel my blood pink
your breasts, crimson your lucid arms.
I want to stir your black silks,
feel men's eyes, women's admiring glances. I want to glide
in your furs down the Rue di Rivoli, swing your cool thighs,
clench your inner lips curled in their black nest between your legs.
I want to die into your arms, cohabit you, leave
my scales and cracks behind.

Rescue me, Madame X, take me out of this body not mine,
reach out your smooth hands, bring me into you, hip to hip,
reach in and rescue me.

I was born to be a beauty, to all the love that comes with loveliness.
Lift me up into you, Madame X,
hold me in your arms as my legs curve into yours.
Reach down and rescue me from staring strangers,
reach down as if you were the Virgin Mother,
reach down and raise me up.

The Empty Chair

Both my poems in this anthology are about the loss of a body I've never had. Not an idealized body, but a normal one, one whose skin is smooth and natural. Because I have had a disorder called ichthyosis since birth, my skin is red, scaly, and tough. I deeply wish I were different— a wish which goes against the credos of disability rights, which ask us to celebrate our differences. The activists, for whom I have a lot of admiration, say it's not the disabled body which is out of synch, but the environment, often the built environment. Not the limp of the man with cerebral palsy, but the unaccommodating architecture and the presupposition of architects that all people who use their buildings can leap up steps as easily as cats chasing birds.

The corollary is for me to persuade myself that my scaly skin is beautiful. I can't do it. Oh, I can see the lovely bone structure of my face, but that comes along with a ferocious redness, well beyond the hues of most people of European descent such as me. So, I am not a poet in the ranks of the orthodox disability rights activists. OK. There's room for all perspectives, although some people would say, with some reason, that my attitude only perpetuates stigmas against people with disorders of the skin. Clearly all this bothers me. I don't want to feel that my work might be dismissed as insufficiently doctrinaire—although honestly, this has not happened. Heaven knows I don't want to internalize stigmas, but there's a difference, I think, between self-hatred and a more cool-headed recognition that my body is not beautiful.

And so, I mourn the loss of an ordinarily attractive body. And in my poetry, I admit to that. I let all those emotions of loss and yearning out. Long ago, when I first started to write poetry, I knew it was necessary to tell the truth of how I felt. I still think that. But there's another question I find tricky: how to end poems? Our culture demands reconciliation, healing. Readers want to feel better about the difficult situations that are revealed in poetry such as mine. I resist the happy ending with every fiber of my poetic being. There is no happy ending in my poems, or, for that matter, perhaps, in my life. And I'll be damned if I am going to impose one on heartfelt yearning.

There is, of course, another way. I can work to make the poem itself as beautiful as I have the talent to manage. Beautiful in its images, sounds, sensuousness. This is balm for me and for my readers. I don't mean to sugar-coat it or make it pretty. But I try to give the reader the kick in the solar plexus which comes from encountering the truth in lines that are both raw and rhythmical, whose well-chosen meters give genuine punch to the ideas and feelings they carry. That's what I'm about as a poet.

In Virginia Woolf's masterpiece *To the Lighthouse*, I find a corollary to my convictions. One of the central characters, Lily Briscoe, is a painter—not a great painter, but a serious one. She is also plain and yearns for the attentions of the beautiful, dominating Mrs. Ramsay, the major character. Mrs. Ramsay, middle-aged mother of a flock of children, wife to a demanding and loving husband, is generally adored by everyone who meets her. I too am attracted to people like Mrs. Ramsay. I too want to be them, or at least like them—loved, powerful, full of life, the center of the mainstream culture in which I live. Near the end of Woolf's book, Lily is out on a lawn, painting what she thinks is an empty chair in the doorway of the Ramsays' house. Suddenly, Mrs. Ramsay moves into the chair. Then a breeze flutters the curtain in front of the window and Lily can see Mrs. Ramsay for a moment. Lily feels utterly abandoned. "'Mrs. Ramsay! Mrs. Ramsay!' she cried, feeling the old horror come back—to want and want and not to have. Could she inflict that still?" I have often thought of these words, this scene. It mirrors the yearning I too have felt for the Mrs. Ramsays in my life. But Lily is not defeated. At the end of the book, she is painting again in the same spot. Mrs. Ramsay is dead—famously killed off by Woolf in a parenthesis in the middle of the novel. Even dead, Mrs. Ramsay can evoke yearning in Lily. Looking toward the house, Lily senses the dead woman's presence in the empty chair. With a stoke of her brush, Lily nails her. "With a sudden intensity, as if she saw it clear for a second, she drew a line there, in the centre. It was done; it was finished. Yes, she thought, laying down her brush in extreme fatigue, I have had my vision." I find this ending thrilling and deeply satisfying. Lily's artistry—or rather Woolf's—gives me what Lily and I, in other senses, don't always get: satisfaction.

Try It Yourself(ie): Yourself as a Tree

Draw yourself as a tree. The quality of the drawing doesn't matter at all. Write about what you see. What are your roots, your branches, your sap? What animals and insects find shelter within you? What shade do you provide? Turn this into a poem.

My Melissa,

whose trans body is a house without a hacksaw, a nap inside

a needle, a glass vase ¾ full of smooth stones;

whose trans aorta is a mesquite tree careening through power lines,
    a Cooper's Hawk

lit by lightning; whose trans lungs are two jars full

of bumblebees singing on the uncovered back porch. Even our name is
    a match

tossed into the fire it started, an edgeless invocation. Melissa, a wind

made by swinging; grass cutting through concrete; bubble-wrap being
    danced on,

albeit slowly, as if that alone could quiet the tiny explosions down the hall.
    Whose

trans articular cartilage is string light threaded through the rafters; whose
    trans

tunica media is a sliver of decorated cardboard doubling as a protest

sign inside the window, which only serves to emphasize the window's
    inefficacy

against the sun; whose trans epiglottis is an apron

on a hook; whose trans trapezius are cups in the sink filled

with inconsistently directed knives and spoons; whose trans metatarsals
    are

green beans boiling on the stove; whose trans subclavian artery is organ

pipe cactus under cloud cover; whose trans left ventricle is a black-capped
    goldfinch
hanging

upside down to eat; whose trans lesser trochanter is a hen's claw growing
    around a rope;

whose trans great saphenous veins are technologies of prediction—tarot,
    storm-

tracker, political polls; whose trans dead space is the undeniable pollution

of light; whose trans thyroid cartilage is commissioned

graffiti; whose trans facial hair is the gentrifier yelling

gentrification; whose trans erythrocytes are dapples of daylight

drug across a concrete block wall; whose trans stroke volume is a live-

streamed filibuster; whose trans plasma is the intimacy

of strangers immediate in an emergency; whose trans plasma proteins are
    women

filling a courtroom—one by one approaching the judge—performing

all the mental and physical labor of obtaining a divorce; whose trans
    integumentary
system

is the myth of meritocracy; whose trans rectum is a local philanthropic
    institution;

whose trans bile is the taste of a slap echoing in your mother's open palm;

whose trans femoral vein is a cat's claw's crafted search for the sun;

whose trans pharynx is an empty building brimming with trampolines;
    whose trans
ovaries

are interrobangs used unironically; whose trans ureter is

a stop sign stuffed with bullet holes near a ditch filled with sunflowers near
    a wasp's

nest near a farm. Sometimes I'm afraid I am afraid

of me, my trans sympathetic nervous

system, my trans fatigue

cracks, my trans 1st Corinthians 3:16 training

the god right out of my trans temple,

all trans dove, no savior; a trans baptism, holy

to be a fire (trans) trembling in the tear of the trans (daughter, trans)
    tongue. How I love
you

now, my trans vagina, my trans manubrium, my trans Melissa, in every iter-
    ation TC

Melissa Dawn Tolbert who was even once

a Harrison, a wife to a husband; it is possible she loved

me then too. Hiding can she hear me

say thank you. To my trans uterus, my trans pectoralis major, my trans pe-
nis: the highest
point

on earth is in the ocean. Sea stars, our body's becoming. A trans prayer. An
infinite,
inexhaustible

rhizome of the heart. You,

whose tragus is trans, whose kidneys, whose medulla oblongata, whose

adrenal glands, whose cochlea, whose pleural space; whose trans sacrum is
simultaneous,

the site of the storm and the keel of a storm-scored boat.

Whose trans arrector pili muscle is the fact that no matter when this sen-
tence is read, it
will be true

that someone somewhere is trying to survive a sexual assault; whose trans
inferior

vena cava is a clock that has not yet been hung on the wall.

I love you time, how trans you are.

Your trans boredom, ribbon-sharp and meadow-bold. You, whose bark is

trans; whose recovery, whose lumen, whose partial pressure

(trans), in order to live, must continue to respond to changes in the lungs.

A man's arms may trick

his shadow—Melissa—may become the open chamber he longs to live
    inside–

held in the lungs of another—what unforetold music may emerge

even from the hair of a horse stretched between two bent ends of a Per-
    nambuco stick and
then

rubbed against a dried and twisted selection of a young sheep's gut—it is
    2019 and

every day now the world's windows rattle—sunrise, that relentless bastard,
    still

searches the dirt for what has the potential to explode—what cannot be-
    come louder larger

if only by eventually allowing itself to be slammed shut—perhaps this is
    another
way of singing into

every day's disappearance—enlarging what survives—without
    justification—here I am
having

never learned how to keep (this too the work of every beating body)
    time—what if we did
not

suspect the dead of going on somewhere without us—would we call our
    own names—
if we knew

the very wind pushing through each fence, each room was to be
    remembered

as another's expelled breath—silent—looking at you now, shaping sound
    strikes me as

departure practice—lifting up from the shoulders a little—listening for
    the measure
marked

tacet—wave after wave expanding against one another—underneath loss
    lives touch—

In someone else's home, 2018 February 08,

you are sitting in front of a considerable yellow mirror. Carved
into the frame of the mirror are flowers, the leaves
of which, were they solo, could be mistaken for thumb-
nails lined up at a salon waiting for the arrival of the hands
to which they should be attached. There are fish under-
water above you trying to tell the night what is coming.
One fish, in particular, has eyelashes and a body covered
in lines much like a topographical map. You remember there
are tiny brooms all over your own skin that, even if you say
stop, will not stop. You have said *stop* so many times before
to your own body, whatever that is, and the lines being drawn
upon it. Now that testosterone has occluded estrogen, there
must be fewer bodies like yours, or more, it's hard to say.
You often mistake reflection for its lyrical sibling and it hurts
to see anything this late. The auburn closet to your right
was built after the room was finished. *Closet* isn't exactly
the right word, but neither is *metal bar with hangers inside
an irregular collection of shelves.* You have always been drawn
to containers, repositories of any kind, strung with a simple strip
of cloth. Perhaps this is why you cannot call Melissa,
or even Missy, your *deadname.* You understand the problems with *birth-
name* and still you've spent so much time bargaining
to believe every name you've ever been called points at least
partially to a body alive that you are willing to love today. The mirror
only returns parts of what holds you to yourself, no matter
the angle, and in this way it is just like language, just
like every story about transition with which you've been
harassed. Faced with the haunting of our innumerable
we become severing. Your prayer was severaled. Like the night
to which you are repeatedly hope-harnessed and into
which soon enough you will pass.

felo-de-se—Melissa

physicists say we change an object simply by turning
our attention to it—really I am a grandson
only when we are eating at Panera—one of us is lying
always about her particular hunger—I love the children outside of me
counting to 30 while covering their eyes—whose body
will we sacrifice to be in the company of another—each
day across my ongoing—I haul the husk of her—fire
towers are designed for distance viewing—and I am right
here—mothering you into the next life—call me cover
when you don't know who I could be—time's
psychologic and legal assault—no one is listening to
ice become water—burying you to keep us alive—

Oct 21, 2020: Mo(u)rning

Just a few weeks ago, I celebrated my fourteenth testostoversary—that is, fourteen years on testosterone. Since we were (and still are) in the midst of COVID times and we live in the desert and for the last four months we've been surrounded by wildfire and seemingly never-ending sun (we broke a record in September for passing one hundred days at one hundred degrees or more this year), my partner and I went in search of hot springs and chilly weather and camping anywhere above five-thousand feet.

In trans communities, it's common to hear talk of *deadnames* (the name a trans person was given at birth and/or a previous name that does not reflect their gender identity—therefore a name no longer in use). When a trans person is referred to by their previous name or their name given at birth, this is called *deadnaming*. But that's not language that resonates with me. Fourteen years ago I wanted to hide Melissa Dawn more than I wanted her dead, so I stood before a judge and asked to have a new first name—TC. An act of protection—from men, from women, from me—tucking Melissa Dawn into the fold of my name, I hid her right there in plain sight.

That said, on my recent testostoversary trip, it was something of a surprise to me that we would wind our way to the place I had taken myself a decade ago, a place where I'd gotten serious about trying to erase my whole life. To survive such intense suicidality four years into my transition—how astounded I am now—wildly humbled and grateful—that in ways I never could have foreseen TC, Melissa, and Dawn are together alive.

The thing about elegies people often forget is the turn toward praise— lament cannot exist without love. I imagine every poem I write to be an elegy (self or otherwise). There's no "going back" to who we were five minutes ago, much less who we were before any significant grief or loss. Knowledge, too, makes something new live and something old die. To be trans, for me, is to be fully present to the simultaneity of dying and coming, finally, to life.

Try It Yourself(ie): A Lament Cannot Exist Without Love

1. Put your face six to eight inches away from a reflective surface of some kind. While attending to your face, say your own name over and over again for five minutes straight. Say your name with every inflection, at every speed, at every pitch, and every shape you can imagine. Follow your own name as it becomes infinitely strange.

2. At the close of every day for one year take five seconds and say out loud: Thank you, body, for staying with me today. Thank you, body, for changing.

3. Write a love poem to your old face.

Bobby Pin

When Louise Brooks pranced in the film *Pandora's Box*,
showing off her helmet hair, its curls sharp
and defiant, as she broke one heart after another,
not quite comprehending the power of her sex,
I thought my future was made. I held the wavy spear
of immorality by keeping my woman's bobbed hair
in place. She drank bad whiskey and laughed
as jazz smoked and snaked through speakeasies.
Then she dared to lift her skirt for a Yale fella
who brushed me off. She forgot to look for me
when I fell into a crack of hardwood floor.
I still call out her name.

Universal Remote Control

Until I am pressed, my life is useless.
My electronic boys by the TV
are too busy grooming their silver sheen
and showing off their LCD blink-bling.
When my beeps turn angry, a shrill fire drill,
I am their mother, and they hate it.
They respond slowly as if they're too cool
to admit that yeah, they have a mother.
They drop their shoulders and move, fast-forward,
to selections on the Blu-Ray disc's menu
as if touching a Lamborghini.
They swagger with grins of insolence.
What they don't know is that they'll die young.
All last-year models do. I soldier on.

Washing Machine

I was a blocky cow who chewed its cud in suds.
My steel dentures were bleached clean with toxins.
My stomach had a strong constitution.
Even animals couldn't survive as long.
When humans stuffed my mouth with dirty clothes,
I learned again their language of sweat and soil.
They emitted the methane of loneliness.
I allowed clumps of dirt to clog the gaps
between my gnarly teeth. It was a sweet grass,
a longing for the days when I could breathe
free of that basement lit by a sad bulb.
I dreamed of pastures greener in the sun,
a pastoral pond lined with lily pads.
Now I'm junked with other useless dreamers.

Self-Objectification

At times, while I was growing up, I felt as if I didn't have a name. I was just a pair of body hearing aids strapped onto my chest. My nasal speech announced to everyone that I was different. I may have had a name, but most hearing people didn't think of my name when they thought of me. They remembered the earmolds that protruded like Frankenstein's creature's bolts out of my head.

It has taken me decades to understand that I had become objectified in their eyes. I wasn't really a person. I was the sum of my hearing aids. I was not "normal," therefore I required endless hours of speech therapy and lip-reading practice, and many admonitions not to learn sign language. I am also sure that my own Catholic mother prayed endless hours for my salvation.

For the longest time I'd unquestioningly adopted her hopes for me to do well as my *modus operandi*. I would become the best student, the best son, and the best altar boy she could ever ask for. I wore her hopes like the virgin-white surplice and black cassock while trying to walk gracefully in a pair of shoes that didn't quite fit me. (The priest had a box full of shoes in varying sizes for us altar boys in the sanctuary, and I was too poor to own a pair of such shoes.)

And for what? I learned American Sign Language (ASL) anyway. Thank God, or I'd have become another suicide casualty of audism and ableism. Sometimes I do mourn how much of my own social potential wasn't developed in those days, and when I do, I have to check my own anger at having been treated as not equal while growing up. I should lament the fact that I no longer seek out my hearing family's love and acceptance, but I don't. I am just a ghost in their midst.

Many people have strong feelings about Madonna, the pop singer and media provocateur, a role she still seems to relish, but aside from that, I do admire how she keeps reinventing herself with each new album.

I try to do the same thing with each of my poetry collections. I want to shake it up all over again when I start a new batch of poems.

I'd done the deaf, oral, and Catholic thing with *St. Michael's Fall*; the nature poems with *This Way to the Acorns*; the Deaf gay experience in *Mute*; the loss of a long-term relationship in *Road Work Ahead*; a psychedelic-like trip through the history of Western poetry with a heavy dosage of climate change and science fiction with *How to Kill Poetry*; and the depiction of Walt Whitman as a gay man so remarkably similar to the social media–addicted gay men of our time with *The Kiss of Walt Whitman Still on My Lips*.

What else could I explore?

In 2007 I edited a piece called "Dining-Room Talk" for my book *When I am Dead: The Writings of George M. Teegarden*. The Deaf writer (1852–1936) had imagined a group of dining room objects having a vivid conversation. That made me wonder what sort of things *I* would say if I were an inanimate object. I decided right then and there to try a series of short object poems; pithiness was a necessary antidote to the wild and ambitious scale of my previous collection *How to Kill Poetry*. (I hadn't written my Whitman book yet.)

Long after I finished *A Babble of Objects*, I began to wonder: why objects? Whatever possessed me to focus on them in the first place? The realization gradually dawned on me: my feelings toward these objects were largely informed by how others had viewed *me* not as a human being but as someone with things in his ears. I was a *thing*, and rather treated as such. (Or put another way: it's much easier to bully and attack someone who seems more like a *thing* rather than a fellow human being just like them.)

Once I understood the subconscious impulse that drove me to complete *A Babble of Objects*, I am shocked by how incredibly personal these object poems have become. Granted, I have never been a washing machine, a bobby pin, or a universal remote control, but each of my objects is saying the same thing: *Listen to me! I have a life. I ache. I exist.*

I think that pressing demand to be heard and respected is most likely true of any disabled person. We are so used to being ignored and objectified long enough to be bullied and taunted that any opportunity to be heard *as we are* and to be appreciated as such becomes truly precious. That is why I continue to write.

I have no interest in mourning what I've lost because of my deafness.

I have no interest in being pigeonholed where I'm not wanted.

I have no interest in pity.

I am not an object.

People already know this about themselves, so why do they keep forgetting this fact when they put us down?

I too am a human being.

After a lifetime of being treated like a second-class citizen even among my own hearing family, I demand to be heard and treated as an equal.

Try It Yourself(ie): Before You Croak

What would you like your last words be before you croak? Takes turns listing serious and funny possibilities. Play up any possible contradictions. Eventually, try moving toward some wisdom you wish to share. Or wisdom you wish had been shared with you sooner. Turn this into a poem.

Murder Defense

I need to make my case. She edits my entries and twists my story to make it fit her survival. I'm a good guy. Not a stalker. Not creepy. She is like one of those breakups where the person says I never liked you to begin with. But she loved me. Wanted the whole package. *She* pursued *me*. Woke me up at all hours. Crisis calls as if I was 911 when my work calls for the coroner, not CPR. She told me I was her last hope, back pocket plan. How is that supposed to make a guy feel? I just tried to meet her needs. Held quick on the roller coaster ride she took me on. In and out of locked hospital wards where she never put me on the visitor list. I worried. Binge-watched *Hinterland*. Took up smoking again. Chewed my nails to the quick. Eventually, she'd be out. Then apology texts. Would I meet for coffee? Forgive her? Even for a job a guy has limits. What I'm trying to say is I put up with a lot. Stayed steady. Kept her in my sights. Didn't waiver in my commitment or resolve. There for her. Still.

Primetime

I sit in my La-Z-Boy and watch myself on the 6 o'clock news. My fifteen minutes. Bagged Kate Spade and Anthony Bourdain. My work is put under the microscopes of cultural critics. I don't pay much attention–career hazard to see the impact to those left behind. Switch to *True Detective* on Netflix and pop a craft ale.

*

There is still my nemesis. She doesn't need me anymore, doesn't want me, stopped calling. Hell, I rarely flit across her brain after being her sole obsession for years. But I know where she lives in her new house with her wife and her dog. Track her successes on social media. She didn't friend me on Facebook, but I have other methods. I still plan to finish the job. Don't like the undone feel. Wakes me up some nights. And, yes, I know I'm supposed to focus on the larger picture. I've been privy to enough therapy sessions that I'm hip to the cognitive all-or-nothing trap. Can keep a gratitude journal until my smile freezes.

*

This was an unusual high profile week so I'm on the down low. I'll stay in this den and make strategic moves from the computer. So many of these pitifuls are already brink and nearly over–no skill involved–just an anonymous bully tweet. The workload is 24/7. Not just around holidays or full moons or in the spring anymore. I've quit my day job as an Eli Lilly drug rep (though similar skills and often the same results). And the young ones–I almost feel a pang for those teens–OD or brain all over from the family gun. I send a regular check to the NRA for making my job easy.

*

She haunts me–the one who slow danced in my grip. I'll wait. In the meantime, I've got several jumpers tonight, barely need to give them a nudge. An inept psychiatrist who just prescribed a 90 day supply of Ambien–call that done. And the suicide helpline with a fresh batch of volunteers. I still do my workouts at the local gym, keep my AR-15 oiled and ready. I have to be prepared for when she calls. Can't get lazy while the world is in apocalypse mode. Climate change, disillusionment, makes my job cake. Call it contract labor, call it an exit service. Evidence-based. Look at the stats. Tenth leading killer in the US. Had to chuckle to myself. Made the top ten list.

Murderer 401K

People ask how I keep up my impeccable record. I'd like to say persistence, dedication, passion, those trademark American work ethic values. But really, it's the easiest job ever. I was made for this. Maybe I should get a better PR agent. Make this look tough: highlight my intensive workout regimen, daily target practice, psychological studies of my clients so I know their tics. I could charge more but figure a life is enough. Some lives are worth more than others, but it balances out in the end. With such high demand and escalating suicide rates, I've played with the idea of expanding: employees, increased revenue, wider service offerings. But I prefer the control of my one-man-murderer-band. I can be selective and only take the difficult cases, leave the rest to the amateurs (luring a person in an extreme mind state to jump off a bridge is below me, pardon the pun). I've thought about retirement. Kick back in the La-Z-Boy a bit more. Take a beach holiday that doesn't involve rocks in pockets, boat "accidents," or unexplained rip currents. Some work is for life, in my case death, and there is no retirement package from who you are.

Murder Witness

These pieces are from my book *Psych Murders,* a hybrid memoir poem that documents my experience of electroconvulsive therapy or shock treatment and shifts in and out of locked psychiatric wards and extreme bipolar mind states. It is often a struggle for me to translate my bipolar experiences to the medical-industrial-complex world and the general population. The time period covered in *Psych Murders* was fraught with intense, relentless suicidal ideation. I wanted to find a way to share the complexity of living with the desire to die without resorting to straight narratives and certainly without the rainbow arc of hopeful endings found in so many memoirs. Enter the Murderer.

The Murderer gave me a device to move suicidal ideation out of my body and into its own agency as a person with choices, feelings, desires. In essence, this is often how suicidal ideation felt in my bodymind; like an intruder that yelled at me to kill myself as I was going through the grocery checkout and doing my best to not do the ultimate checkout. The act of personifying suicidality gave me room to relate to and try to understand this character. The complexity within my love-hate relationship and mixed interior and exterior messages with suicidality became more apparent. I didn't want to kill myself, yet I was in such a deep depression and/or mixed state (depth of depression combined with agitation and impulsiveness of mania, considered a very high-risk state for suicide) that I didn't want that exit blocked.

The elegiac nature of these poems resides partly in the act of me being alive to write them. Suicidal ideation, or the Murderer, never realized himself and his purpose. (I use the pronouns he/him intentionally as the Murderer in the poems manifested as a male figure. I also use male gender to mark psychiatry's history and current practices that more often than not have men diagnosing women and queer and trans folx as sick. Not to mention that all of my shock "treatments" were performed by male doctors.) The Murderer in these pieces didn't get to live fully and perform his function, to kill me. He may still be around and waiting for an opportunity, but for all purposes, the narrator has moved on with her life and no longer thinks about him much.

If someone being dead is part of a traditional elegy, then in these poems the Murderer does indeed die or become unnecessary, inconsequential. The reality for me and the many people who identify as Mad is that suicidal ideation and extreme bodymind states can and do return. This shadow of possibility in some ways mimics death in a traditional elegy. We mourn the death of the subject of the elegy while also mourning our own mortality. The Murderer is actually bummed out that I don't pay attention to him anymore and didn't even accept his Facebook friend request.

In this anthology's focus on self-elegy, I resonate with the idea of a part of the self dying. In this case, it is a destructive part of me and the result of extreme bodymind states. Unlike a traditional elegy where the writer is mourning the death of the subject of the poem, these self-elegies lean into the transformation and freedom enabled by the loss. The Murderer perhaps could write a lament about how much he misses who I used to be when we danced together in a complicated life/death two-step. Fortunately, I have less remorse and am grateful to move through my days and the grocery checkout without 24/7 suicidal ideation.

These poems gave me the opportunity to reflect and heighten my awareness of my relationship with suicide. I think one of the most important things that self-elegy offers is the opportunity to witness. By personifying the Murderer, I was able to better understand the motivations and the security provided by suicidal ideation. I was surprised by the dark, sardonic humor that emerged in the Murderer. He indeed presented himself like the protagonist in a noir film. I never imagined writing about suicide and having parts of it be funny. When I performed these at a poetry reading, I had someone share afterwards that they wanted to laugh but weren't sure it was appropriate. I want that tension and want my readers to have their own gestalt experience of these pieces. My intention in this work is not only to witness my own experience but also to convey and translate that experience. I hope humor, albeit dark humor, offers a little more space to engage with this difficult and often deadly topic.

I chose these pieces, all from the perspective of the Murderer, in part because they illustrate my shift from past self, dependent on my relationship with the Murderer ("*She told me I was her last hope, back pocket plan*"), to present survivor self, where the Murderer is no longer central ("*She doesn't need me anymore, doesn't want me, stopped calling"*). And yet, the Murderer still has me in his sights. I hope to emphasize the interdependence and precarity of living in relationship with the Murderer. To stay alive, there are inevitably other supports at play, be they loved ones, peers, mental health professionals. (And I hesitate to put psych wards on this list, as I'm firmly in the antipsychiatry camp, yet I'm not sure I'd be here without psychiatric hospitalizations when I needed a break from negotiating with the Murderer and a place where it was easier to not act on suicidal impulses. Simultaneously, I believe we need new paradigms to replace the prison psychiatric complex.)

This list of supports also includes the Murderer. Suicidal ideation is a much more common and frequent experience than most would like to acknowledge among both Mad people and people who don't identify around mental health difference at all. The important part of writing *Psych Murders* was to convey for myself and readers that multiple futures, multiple ways of being, living, and thriving, are possible. And this includes futures with the Murderer. I couldn't, in good conscience, conclude with a whip cream topping of hope where the Murderer is completely out of the picture, and the narrator is magically rid of or (it's a miracle!) cured. My writing and life aim to celebrate and embrace the ebbs and flows of shifting bodymind states.

Try It Yourself(ie)

Exits & Entrances

Take an inventory of what you'd like to let go of in your life. This could be a habit, emotion, situation, possession, quality. Witness what arrives and take a couple minutes to jot it down in whatever format resonates with you (on computer, phone, notebook, drawing paper, etc.). Now shift gears and spend time with what you'd like to welcome into or amplify in your life. Make a separate list.

Breakup Letter

Review what you want to let go of and pick the item that has the most energy/juice. Let yourself be surprised. Write a letter directly addressing it, explaining why you can't have it in your life anymore. You might include what it offered you in the past, gratitude for how this thing served you, but that now you need to end it. Be clear on the future terms of contact or lack of contact. Have fun with creating a character. For example, I might write a letter to procrastination and complain about how I can't handle their half-drunk coffee cups all over the house or the fact they are always in my favorite chair.

Personal Ad

Pick something you want to usher into your life from your list. Write an advertisement for it including what specifically you are looking for, why now, and what you have to offer. Include as much detail as possible. Imagine how they smell, what they eat for breakfast, what makes them laugh. What makes you a good match for them? You might even look at some personal ads to get an idea for the particular vocabulary of this form.

Deadly Doll Head Dissection

Doll head fantasyland, fun-filled dollies, licking dollies, slurping dollies, yummy dollies, gummy dollies, genuflecting dollies, dick sucking dollies, doll gags, doll debauchery, a sipping, slipping, discombobulated dolly.

A doll thought she was being drunk sweetly. A doll thought she was softly peeking, but she was peaking like an anorexic doll head turning black. Like a servile ugly duckling with a deviated septum soon to be a cunt doll, an asshole doll, a stinky dolly douche bag, a bitchy doll injection mold disaster. Bleeding doll, broken doll, doll head rape. Shackled doll, spasmed doll, mangled doll, impaled doll, unglued doll legs, smashed doll brain.

Deadly doll head dissection. A dolly crematorium, an almost life less doll. A doll scatterbrained, a doll agitating until it barfs up more awful doll head gobbledygook. A spitting and hacking doll. Spinning, falling and flailing inside the doll vomitorium. A dark doll somnambulating and throwing up.

A doll hurling jerky truffles, a doll unfurling quirky squiggles. A scary doll giggles then explodes like a dollcano. A bloody shimmering doll. A hotly whirring doll. A rising up doll head. A transforming doll brain. A doll biting back until penile balloons hiss then deflate . . .

Self Portrait as a Slab on a Slab

I'm a little slice of pound cake in a little coffin,
served with a little container of half & half.
Where will you pour the creamer?

I'm a cut off braid with silver threads,
served on a silver platter. Split ends
unloose themselves from multiple strands.

I'm a slab on a slab, a plait on a plate,
a poorly shorn lamb on the lam.
I'm sweet, heavy, deathly, hairy.
I'm shaved, heaving, dripping, dirty
with my ruffled bloomers torn off
at the stems. So throw me in. Fast forward

my declension. Will I thrash or gulp?
Will I sink or float? Will I suck it all up
like a sugary sea sponge with teeth?

Un-sided Self Portrait

My red yarn brings all the boys to the yard
and then sinks them down under the buoys.

My dark crystals are hidden inside
sunken ravens.

Just because I sink down
doesn't mean I still can't swim
in my own directions.

Doesn't mean I still can't maneuver up.
Maybe I just don't want to
with you.

Some of you take sides too quickly,
as if there are only two.
I'm a many sided protrusion.

Sometimes I like to keep
the positive parts to myself
and only release the negatives.

I can sink myself, keep my own
glitter under wet ashes,
until I decide to rise it up.

Broken Doll Hands that had to Grow New Fingers

'm a middle-aged, middle-class, disabled white woman. I look older than I feel. Sometimes I don't feel as if there's anything very meaningful about me, except when I'm expressing myself via art and poetry. Sometimes I feel as if my art and poetry is relatively meaningless on a larger scale too. Sometimes I feel as if there is no larger scale and I try my best to remain focused on my own small scale.

I was the oldest of four children, grew up with a loving, caring family, but in my teenage years, I self-interpreted my upbringing as overprotective and somewhat controlling, unintentionally causing me to feel as if the real me was not appreciated on an individual level. I felt the need to attempt to express my real self in a very individualistic way, including on paper filled with my own forms of personal expression, so that I would grow into my true self and exist somewhere other than inside my own mind. In retrospect, I might have mostly just been expressing my own mind to myself, but that led to my own mind's personal growth.

For several years in my late teens/early twenties, I had a fear that I might be a writer who would die young, before I had reached the ability of being able to express my true self as well as I wanted to. I also had trouble visually seeing myself. Throughout most of my twenties, I looked in the mirror too much, not because I thought I was particularly attractive, but because my mind had trouble visualizing myself unless I continually looked at myself. Whenever I was sitting in a group, my mind tried to convince me I was invisible to others and didn't exist as an individual. In my early thirties, when I acquired my first digital camera, I took selfie after selfie, to visually analyze my own appearance and my own self.

In my early to mid-thirties, after years of working to hone my own writing skills, I was extremely excited that my poetry finally began to emerge more naturally and genuinely and even semiautomatically. Then at thirty-seven,

I suffered from a stroke, had to relearn the alphabet, couldn't understand my own poems, but could certainly remember my own genuine passion for creative words and relied upon that to help the words reemerge. I feel that my genuine passion for poetry and in-depth personal expression played a hugely significant role in my recovery from the stroke's side effects, but I also felt like I might be boring other people by repeatedly talking about that. Now I'm in my mid-forties and even though I appreciate my different life experiences, I still often question my own value and relevance.

The poems I'm submitting to this anthology all appear within my second full-length poetry collection, *Malformed Confetti.* The collection is divided into five different sections and includes poems from 2008 to 2014. My age range during that time frame was thirty-five to forty and, in the midst of that time, some significant life changing and brain changing experiences occurred. It was at the beginning of 2010 that I had an unexpected carotid artery dissection, which led to an aneurysm, which led to a stroke, which resulted in brain damage and aphasia and which also seemed to result in my divorce exactly one year later. Although I don't regret the divorce, the rather sudden unexpected succession of brain damage followed by divorce increased my self-doubt, lack of trust in relationships, and difficulty believing in or trusting love or knowing how to interpret it. Different variations on that seemed to infiltrate a lot of my poetry for about five years, the same number of years that I was married. But even before that, for years I've often felt as if I'm losing my appeal in one way or another (and as if I will never be anyone's favorite thing), so maybe that was a mental glitch of mine to begin with that seemed to be further exacerbated by my brain damage and then my divorce.

My poem "Deadly Doll Head Dissection" is mentally linked to my stroke, the resultant brain damage, and my divorce, but in a rather abstract and mental sort of way. I remember when I was working on writing it, I felt that it probably was not going to make much sense to anyone else, content-wise (and that it might be perceived as absurdly grotesque borderline silly)—but whether or not others understand its content, I know how it felt to me. It's about self-deprecation, self-abuse, abuse by others, thinking I deserved it, thinking it was my fault, breakage, brain damage, and then challenging realignment. Attempting to turn my physical and mental disabilities into rage that fights back against what tries to break me down. My brain was brimming with broken doll hands that had to grow new fingers and I managed to grow them back; but now what do they mean?

Although I've always felt drawn towards exploring and expressing and questioning myself as an individual, in recent years I find myself occasionally questioning the redundancy of my own self-expression. I'm a woman who has spent more than twenty-five years trying to focus on my own creative process and expression—to what end? I still question myself and doubt myself and my own validity and lucidity. Maybe I'm too self-focused, maybe I'm not direct enough, maybe I'm a repetitive contradictory mess, maybe I'm an ongoing plateau, maybe I'm too uncaring on a large scale. I've always had a small-scale sort of focus. I'm brimming with mixed feelings and not very good at taking sides. I have my own genuine thoughts and feelings, but for the most part, I've never felt very black and white, or right and wrong, or felt like telling others what they should or shouldn't do, or like stating my thoughts/feelings/opinions like they're obvious facts that should make sense to everyone. I don't expect to make sense to everyone; I just try my best to openly, honestly express how I genuinely feel and hope that a few other people might relate to or respect or appreciate what I creatively share.

Try It Yourself(ie): Word Control

Pick a word that bothers you (because you think it's overused, because you think it's repeatedly used in the wrong way, because it upsets you on a personal level, or for some other reason of your own) and use that word in a poem (or several poems) so that you can take control of how that word is used (or redirect how it is used) for your own chosen reasons, rather than hearing other people overuse it and feeling bothered and out of control. Or write about something that angers you. Write about something that scares you. Write about something that's hard for you to write about.

Why Storms are Named After People &
Bullets Remain Nameless

I reach out in love, my hands are guns, my good intentions are
completely lethal. — Margaret Atwood

My body is a canvas. He painted
my eyes as hurricanes swelling with questions. I never ask–
which brush is your favorite? Or,

one day *when you paint my heart
outside of my body will you use all of your favorite colors?* Only the best ones
cover up a vessel's holes,

storm torn linen stretched too thin.
Modern-day marksman, Orion-the-hunter, finger on trigger.
My eyes hold his in orbit:

Look at me, too afraid. He will get lost there.
So I pluck my eyes from skull. *Teach me how to breathe the colors
I could never see without you.*

Unintended impact. His stray-bullet-heart
ricocheted into mine like a painting we didn't mean to step into
with Sagittarius pulling back

bow to enough tension to hold
this milky way's center. Take aim, fire–an arrow across a universe
where we spiral together through

the time we wish we had
more (or less) of. There, we'll rediscover open wounds. Longing
for closure, his mouth opens–

I like the way you fit inside me,
without want. But, I wanted us to fall without loss, domino-effect,
arms outstretched, trust

fall, open, graceful. In another life
we drank in all of the constellations, tasted each star, then committed
light to memory

so we could always navigate our way
back to each other. He will leave me on a starless night. When I wake
I'll find my eyes inside an ashtray

burning, beside his
goodbye note: *Tell me you'll never forget this. Your love is a universe*
too big, too innocent.

Before the sun rises, I'll place my eyes back,
inside out. I want to see everything I was ever afraid of. I want
to know what to (if I should) name him.

A Song for Redemption

My mouth is a cave, calloused with housing your name.
    The overgrowth molds the air. I inhale
    our memories slowly in
and out through lips parted

    open. This is how we lived–
    breaking like orange peel skin, edges inexact
    and me trying to stitch jagged scraps.
    Who was the last
    to suckle sweetness, mouth around flesh?
    The juice of everything I never told you
    inching down my chin.

Imagine this overflowing:
    light exploding as a thousand stars
    sentenced themselves to the ocean. After you
    died, I drank in waves–
        tried flooding my veins to change
    my inner landscape. Guilt.
    I drowned, swallowed mouthfuls,
    until I became drunk on ghosts.

Your name haunts the tip of my tongue.
    A survivor's guilt lump takes root in
    my throat's stem, threatening to explode
    the cold I've learned to live with.

    My heart named itself a stray
    bullet, intent on rediscovering all the holes
    no song was big enough to stop the bleeding–
    heart, yours a black hole
            I spent nights trying to love out of you.
    My fingers couldn't grasp its edges
      so I used my voice to unzip each scar

to climb inside your fear. I found us there
continuously swimming from shore through sea
just to be caught two-stepping on the fiery ship's deck
while the radio plays our favorite song,
the one with the voice grainy–
breadcrumbs we can trace our way back
through any river, city, landscape, or

ruin. I can still taste the sound
in the search for redemption
(mouth full of ash) now I know
what it's like to burn beautifully.

Each Year I Travel Through

Year One.

I pass the line of semis carrying a bridge just before entering a city named
Echo.

I wish I knew what it meant to connect and be connected.

So I roll down all the windows and whisper into the wind– *what are you so
afraid of?*

Year Two.

I keep hoping one day I'll hear my voice travel back to me.

Instead, I teach my students how to hold words in pieces: sound, history,
impact, and beginnings.

Take for instance *colonized*. Etymology. Colon: body politik. Imagine it in-
side your body, a snake swallowing everything.

Year Three.

Someone who once took my love wrote to me: *Love is a verb. Our existence
is verbing.*

I said *took* but I should really say *stole*.

Year Four.

I have been undoing ever since. Trying to write my way back to a begin-
ning. So I recall an end. The memory of the year when he told me he
wanted to travel backwards like an echo finding its way back to a throat's
cavern.

I can't remember the exact words he used when he left me but flies circled
our table like vultures. They sounded what I was too afraid to admit.

This love was rotting.

Year Five.

The stench swallowed everything.

Year Six.

Remember: from Latin *rememorari*, meaning *"recall to mind"*

The 1st time I taught poetry the students kicked a blackbird outside on the
grass. I saw them through the window and ran out to stop them. It was
already dead but I asked anyway: *why would you do that?*

They said, *pain demands to be felt.*

Year Seven.

Pain was holding myself in pieces:

> Black feathers on the ground like petals
> plucked from their center pulled off one by one,
> year by year. Post-wish dandelion seeds scattered
> into the wind like parachutes awaiting
> the impact of falling.

Year Eight

Healing was pain, asking: *Can you feel me?*

Year Nine

Name it.
Then choose to let go.   Let go.   Let go.

Year Ten

If I close my eyes I can see a window. On the other side I am a child play-
ing, happy, laughing, and free. I feel the magic and light I was before
pieces of me were stolen, then carried away.

I see me.

I am swinging, kicking my legs up until my feet touch sky. I am imagining
I am going to fly. Before I jump, I whisper to my child self: *It's okay. It's
okay to fall. And when you get lost, remember–*

Love returns in pieces.

Don't be afraid.

One day, you'll find words

for everything.

The Shape (and Choice) of Love

I'd like to think my story is always beginning, that I am always becoming. Each day I learn something new, a soul lesson. These lessons are often about the world around me, the people I interact with, new realizations the people I love(d), and more importantly, the lessons I learn about myself—the ways I navigate this living.

Some lessons unwrap beautifully like poetry, like light reflecting off water, acting as a much-needed mirror to reflect back all the light we cannot always see on our own. Others roll in like thunder, they storm their way into your heart until it floods, washing away everything you thought you knew about life and love. Your heartscape is forever changed.

My ruminations on love flow in and out of my mind like waves crashing into the foundation of my self-learning. These reflections are elegy, the ways I mourn my past demons, ruptures, and all the parts of me I have lost, misplaced, or forgotten along the way. I grieve the pieces hoping my grief is so strong it can *will* the broken back together.

It can take a matter of seconds to shatter something. But, how long does it take to put something (someone) back together?

What kind of magic does it take to weave different timelines together to create a new path?

Perhaps love is the only force capable of this. Perhaps poetry is a tool one can wield to allow us to speak to our past, present, and future selves. Self-love then becomes lamenting the parts of us that have rotted beyond repair. It means nurturing but it also means letting go. Self-love is self-elegy.

As an Indigenous womxn writer who also struggles balancing living in two cultural worlds and confronts colonialism daily, my work doesn't always follow a linear path. I exist outside of spaces society tries to define for me. Love exists outside of time and space and so any work that interrogates, plays with, and expands our knowing if its universal force pulls me in at my heartstrings.

As a poet, I am pulled into moments. Whenever I feel lost in orbit, I gravitate to memory, the timeline of lessons learned in rupture. It was rupture that forced me to find poetry and healing that asked me to write.

In 2007, I lost a friend to suicide. After he took his life, I fell into a grief with depths I never knew existed. In that darkness I listened to "*Goodbye My Lover*" on repeat, my mind went in circles of questioning his suicide, the why's, and the how's. I drowned in those whirlpools of grief and guilt that I could have done something to stop that storm before it wrecked everyone who loved him.

This is the point in my timeline where metaphysical poetry saved me. In 2007, at twenty-two years of age, I'd taken an independent study on John Donne and Wallace Stevens. I became obsessed with "The Snow Man" and contemplated my own coldness, "one must have a mind of winter / to regard the frost and the boughs." Everything was connected and you could feel it, see it, even hear it if you became "the listener, who listens in the snow, / And, nothing himself, beholds / Nothing that is not there and the nothing that is." Trying to understand loss, death, grieving felt like an abyss, like whitespace, like holding everything and nothing all at once.

So I turned to Donne and his *Holy Sonnets* particularly "Death, be not proud," with the famous lines we all know too well "And death shall be no more; Death, thou shalt die." I first learned form from Eavan Boland during my Introduction to Poetics class. I often return to "The Making of a Poem" by Mark Strand and Eavan Boland whenever I need to *feel form* again (if that makes sense). In the history of a sonnet's form, the book describes its shape:

> One strong opening statement of eight lines is followed by a resolution to the emotional or intellectual question of the first part of the poem. This shape made the sonnet a self-sufficient form, open to shades of mood and tone. . . . The powerful and enriching development of the sonnet in the English language certainly owes something to the fact that it presented poets with this choice. On the one hand, there was the Shakespearean sonnet, with its three quatrains and final couplet, which allowed a fairly free association of images to develop lyrically toward a conclusion. Or there was the Petrarchan sonnet as Milton used it in "On His Blindness," with all the dignity of proposal and response.

As human beings we are all self-sufficient forms. We live, we learn, we lose, and eventually we move on from this world. But, I wonder, what are the shapes of grief, loss, and love? As an artist I give form to my poetry each time I organize lines into their rooms, stanzas of understanding. I consciously think about where I break a line because in life, I don't always get to choose my breaking points (these are often discovered along the way). We don't always get to choose what happens to us, but we can choose the way we see or perceive it. This is an elegy of the self.

Time. I have such a complicated relationship with time. Often, we feel like there isn't enough of it. Time to sleep, exercise, work, breathe, laugh, and love. But, time also gifts. In its passage, time provides perspective. Perspective is how we survive.

I am grateful for the reminder in the power of poetry. "Love after love" by Derek Walcott is an excellent example of self-elegy.

> The time will come
>> when, with elation,
>> you will greet yourself arriving
>> at your own door, in your own mirror,
>> and each will smile at the other's welcome,
> and say, sit here. Eat.
>> You will love again the stranger who was your self.
>> Give wine. Give bread. Give back your heart
>> to itself, to the stranger who has loved you
> all your life, whom you ignored
>> for another, who knows you by heart.
>> Take down the love letters from the bookshelf,
> the photographs, the desperate notes,
>> peel your own image from the mirror.
>> Sit. Feast on your life.

And so, here I sit, greeting myself at the door, with the words and poetry that has always been the familiar stranger at my heart of hearts reminding me that some lessons come softly, others burn like wild fire and these are often the most important lessons because they come so intensely and quickly, but they always present you with a choice. Become engulfed by the flames and burn, then wait to rise born anew from the ashes. Or, transform into flame, becoming the fire itself. You can choose to be a fire burning brightly, igniting healing and passion into other hearts because you survived the very elements that tried to defeat you.

It's about practicing love (for yourself, the journey, the path) and acceptance. You learn from the past and you let go of what doesn't serve you because there is never a reason to keep something or someone who is incapable of holding all the wonderful, overflowing light you are. I am grateful for the path and the lessons of the past. I am ever grateful for poetry that allows me to revisit moments however briefly because I know: while some moments may be heartbreakingly beautiful, you're not always meant to live there. Self-elegy doesn't mean staying, it means endlessly moving forward.

Try It Yourself(ie): Reclaiming Your Spirit

What are the parts of you that have been taken from you, shook from you, or stolen from you? Your confidence? Pride? The way you used to dance or love yourself? Write a list of all the traits or characteristics that you used to have but no longer do. Then write "I miss _____" before those traits. For example, "I miss the way I used to dance uninhibited," "I miss the way I used to shine, unafraid to show my true skin." Then mine your list and sentences for phrases or seeds to create a poem that reclaims all of those memories because all of those things are still a part of you. You never lost those things. Your spirit is precious and sacred. No matter what is done to you, nothing can touch your spirit.

ACKNOWLEDGMENTS

Carol Berg's poem "9 Meadowview Road" appeared in *Naugatuck River Review*. Her poem "The Ornithologist Searches for a Shared Ancestry" appeared in *Heron Tree* and in *The Ornithologist Poems* (dancing girl press 2015). Her poem "Abandoned Girl is Full of Words" appeared in *Zone:3*.

Sheila Black's poems "Vivisection," "Velvet and Pins," and "Patriarchy" appeared in *Radium Dream* (Salmon Poetry Ireland 2022). "Self as Last Call" and "A Whale-Like Singing" appeared in *New World Writing*.

Bruce Bond's poem "Refugee" was published in *Frankenstein's Children* (Lost Horse Press 2018).

Kristy Bowen's poem "dear imaginary daughter, (#1)" appeared in *White Stag* Editor Issue April 2018.

Juliet Cook's poems "Deadly Doll Head Dissection," "Self Portrait as a Slab on a Slab," and "Un-sided Self Portrait" all appeared in her second full-length poetry book, *Malformed Confetti* (Crisis Chronicles Press 2018). "Self Portrait as a Slab on a Slab" was also previously published in the Self Portrait Issue of *Poets and Artists*. "Un-sided Self Portrait" was also previously published in *Hermeneutic Chaos Journal* (now defunct).

Adam Crittenden's poem "Devil Dog Road" was published in *Radar Poetry*, issue 13.

Jehanne Dubrow's poem "Self-Portrait with Cable News, Graffiti, Weather" appeared in *Wild Kingdom* (LSU Press 2021).

Stephanie Heit's poems "Murder Defense," "Primetime," and "Murderer 401K" appeared in *Psych Murders* (Wayne State University Press 2022).

Kasey Jueds's poems "Robe," "The Missing Women," and "Keeper" appeared in *Keeper* (University of Pittsburgh Press 2013).

Teresa Leo's poem "Singularity" appeared in *Provincetown Arts* (2018). Her poems "The Heart Has the Capacity to Break and Reset a Million Times" and "Chaos Theory" were published in *Bloom in Reverse* (University of Pittsburgh Press 2014).

Denise Leto's "Postcard Divinations" was first published in *Posit: A Journal of Literature and Art* and was first performed at the Disembodied Poetics Conference at Naropa University.

Raymond Luczak's poems "Washing Machine," "Universal Remote," and "Bobby Pin" were published in *A Babble of Objects* (Fomite Press 2018).

Kyle McCord's poem "Chemo" appeared in the *Indiana Review* and his poem "Self-Portrait at 18 seen at 30" appeared in the *Kenyon Review*.

Carl Phillips's poem "Minotaur" was published in *Rock Harbor* (2003) and his poem "The Smell of Hay" was published in *Riding Westward* (2007).

Kevin Prufer's poem "Giving It Back" was published in *National Anthem.* "Churches" was published in *Churches.* "Immortality Lecture" was published in *How He Loved Them* (Four Way Books). "A Body of Work" appears in *The Fears* (Copper Canyon 2023)

TC Tolbert's poem "My Melissa" was previously published in *POETRY*, May 2020. "In someone else's home, 2018 February 8," was previously published in *American Poetry Review* 48, no. 3. "felo-de-se Melissa" was previously published in *The Nation*, July 15–22, 2019.

Tanaya Winder's poem "Why Storms are Named After People & Bullets Remain Nameless" appeared in *Strange Horizons*, January 2017. Her poem "A Song for Redemption" appeared in *Connotation Press*, May 2018. "Each Year I Travel Through" appeared in *Why Storms are Named After People & Bullets Remain Nameless* (CreateSpace Independent Publishing Platform 2017).

Jane Wong's "Elegy for the Selves" was originally published in *Laurel Review*, and also appeared in *Overpour* (Action Books 2016). "Lessons on Lessening" was originally published in *The Adroit Journal* and appeared in *How to Not Be Afraid of Everything* (Alice James 2021).

Carol Berg's poems were published in *Gyroscope, Crab Creek Review* (Poetry Finalist 2017), *DMQ Review, Hospital Drive* (Contest Runner-Up 2017), *Sou'wester, Spillway, Redactions, Radar Poetry, Verse Wisconsin*. She has two chapbooks, *Her Vena Amoris* (Red Bird Chapbooks) and *"Self-Portraits" in Ides* (Silver Birch Press). She was winner of a scholarship to Poets on the Coast and a recipient of a Finalist Grant from the Massachusetts Cultural Council.

Lauren Berry's first collection, *The Lifting Dress* (Penguin 2011), was selected by Terrance Hayes to win the National Poetry Series prize. Her second collection, *The Rented Altar*, won the C&R Press Award in poetry (C&R Press 2020) and the 2021 gold medal from the Independent Publisher Book Awards. She teaches AP English Literature at YES Prep Public Schools, a charter school that provides college preparatory education to Houston's most underserved communities. Additionally, Lauren leads poetry workshops for local nonprofits Inprint and Grackle and Grackle.

Sheila Black is the author, most recently of the chapbook *All the Sleep in the World* (Alabrava Press 2021). Her fifth collection, *Radium Dream,* was published by Salmon Poetry in 2022. Poems and essays have appeared in *Poetry, Kenyon Review Online, Blackbird, The Birmingham Review, the New York Times,* and elsewhere. She lives in San Antonio, Texas and is a cofounder of Zoeglossia, a nonprofit that works to build a community for poets with disabilities.

Bruce Bond is the author of thirty books including, most recently, *Plurality and the Poetics of Self* (Palgrave 2019), *Words Written Against the Walls of the City* (LSU Press 2019), *Scar* (Etruscan 2020), *Behemoth* (New Criterion Prize, Criterion Books 2021), *The Calling* (Parlor 2021), *Patmos* (Juniper Prize, UMass Press 2021), *Liberation of Dissonance* (Nicholas Schaffner Award for Literature in Music, Schaffner Press 2022), *Choreomania* (MadHat 2022), *Invention of the Wilderness* (LSU Press 2022), *The Mirror, the Patch, the Telescope* (coauthor, David Keplinger; MadHat, forthcoming), and *Therapon* (coauthor, Dan Beachy-Quick; Tupelo Press, forthcoming).

239

Kristy Bowen is a writer and book artist. She creates a regular series of chapbook, zine, and artist book projects. She is the author of several full-length poetry/prose hybrid collections, including the recent *sex & violence* (Black Lawrence Press 2020) and two self-issued volumes, *feed* and *dark country*. She runs dancing girl press & studio.

John Chávez is a professional writer, editor, teacher, and poet. His poetry has appeared in *Copper Nickel, Diode, Notre Dame Review, Puerto del Sol, Palabra,* and *Poet Lore,* among others. He is the author of the chapbook *Heterotopia,* published by Noemi Press, and a coauthor of the collaborative chapbook *I, NE: Iterations of the Junco,* published by Small Fires Press. His first full-length collection, *City of Slow Dissolve,* was published by University of New Mexico Press in 2012 and won the IPPY (Independent Publisher Book Award) Gold Medal for Poetry. He also is coeditor of *Angels of the Americlypse: An Anthology of New Latin@ Writing,* published in 2014 by Counterpath Press.

Juliet Cook's poetry has appeared in a small multitude of print and online publications. She is the author of numerous poetry chapbooks, recently including *Another Set of Ripped-Out Bloody Pigtails* (The Poet's Haven 2019), *The Rabbits with Red Eyes* (Ethel Zine & Micro-Press 2020), and *Histrionics Inside my Interior City* (part of Ghost City Press's 2020 Summer Micro-Chapbook Series). Cook's first full-length individual poetry book, *Horrific Confection,* was published by BlazeVOX. Her most recent full-length individual poetry book, *Malformed Confetti,* was published by Crisis Chronicles Press in 2018. Cook's tiny independent press, Blood Pudding Press, sometimes publishes hand-designed poetry chapbooks and sometimes creates other art. Find out more at JulietCook.weebly.com.

Adam Crittenden was awarded an Academy of American Poets Prize. His writing has appeared in *Barrelhouse, Bayou Magazine, Tupelo Quarterly, Barn Owl Review, Whiskey Island, Quarterly West,* and other journals. *Blood Eagle* is his first full-length book of poetry and is available from Gold Wake Press. Currently, he teaches writing at Central New Mexico Community College.

Kara Dorris is the author of two poetry collections: *Have Ruin, Will Travel* (Finishing Line Press 2019) and *When the Body is a Guardrail* (2020). She has also published five chapbooks including *Carnival Bound [or, please unwrap me]* (The Cupboard Pamphlet 2020). Her poetry has appeared in *Prairie Schooner, DIAGRAM, Harpur Palate, Cutbank, The Tulane Review,* and

Crazyhorse, among other literary journals, as well as the anthology *Beauty is a Verb* (Cinco Puntos Press 2011). Her prose has appeared in *Wordgathering*, *Waxwing*, and the anthology *The Right Way to be Crippled and Naked* (Cinco Puntos Press 2016). She is an assistant professor of English at Illinois College. For more information, please visit karadorris.com.

Jehanne Dubrow is the author of nine poetry collections, including most recently *Wild Kingdom* (LSU Press 2021), and two books of creative non-fiction. Her work has appeared in *POETRY*, *The New England Review*, and *The Southern Review*. She is a professor of creative writing at the University of North Texas.

Floydd Michael Elliott is the author of the poetry collection *The Cloud Can Die Now* and the short story collection *The Horned Melon*.

Rigoberto González is the author of five books of poetry, most recently *The Book of Ruin*, published by Four Way Books. His twelve books of prose include two bilingual children's books, the three young adult novels in the Mariposa Club series, and the memoir *Butterfly Boy: Memories of a Chicano Mariposa*, which received the American Book Award from the Before Columbus Foundation. The recipient of Guggenheim, Lannan, NEA, and USA Rolón fellowships, a NYFA grant in poetry, the Lambda Literary Award for Poetry, the Shelley Memorial Award from the Poetry Society of America, and the Barnes & Noble Writer for Writers Award, he is contributing editor for *Poets & Writers Magazine*. Currently, he is professor of English and director of the MFA Program in Creative Writing at Rutgers-Newark, the State University of New Jersey.

Stephanie Heit is a queer disabled poet, dancer, and teacher of somatic writing and contemplative movement practices. She is a Zoeglossia Fellow, bipolar, and a member of the Olimpias, an international disability performance collective. Stephanie's hybrid memoir poem, *Psych Murders* (Wayne State University Press 2022), dares the reader to ride the jolt of experimental writing that witnesses and survives shock treatments, psychiatric wards, and suicidal ideation toward new futures of care. Her poetry collection, *The Color She Gave Gravity* (The Operating System 2017), explores the seams of language, movement, and mental health difference. She codirects Turtle Disco, a somatic writing space, with her wife and collaborator, Petra Kuppers. For more, see stephanie-heit.com.

Kasey Jueds is the author of two collections of poetry, both from the University of Pittsburgh Press: *Keeper*, which won the 2012 Agnes Lynch Starrett Prize, and *The Thicket*. Her work can be found in journals including *American Poetry Review, Crazyhorse, Narrative, Beloit Poetry Journal, Ninth Letter, Cincinnati Review, Bennington Review*, and *Pleiades*.

Anne Kaier's *How Can I Say It was Not Enough?* won a Propel Poetry Award (Nine Miles Books, 2023). Her essays appear in *About Us: Essays from the Disability Series of the New York Times, 1966journal, Alaska Quarterly Review, Kenyon Review* and other venues. "Maple Lane" was mentioned on the list of Notables in the 2014 edition of *Best American Essays*. Excerpts from her memoir-in-progress appeared in *The Woven Tale* and *The Gettysburg Review*. Her short memoir, *Home with Henry*, is out from PS Books. She has been interviewed on NPR and has been a Fellow at the Virginia Center for the Creative Arts. Sample essays and poems at AnneKaier.com.

Catherine Kyle is the author of *Fulgurite* (Cornerstone Press, 2023), *Shelter in Place* (Spuyten Duyvil 2019), which received an honorable mention for the Idaho Book of the Year Award, and other poetry collections. Her writing has appeared in *Bellingham Review, Mid-American Review, The Pinch*, and other journals, and has been honored by the Idaho Commission on the Arts, the Alexa Rose Foundation, and other organizations. She was the winner of the 2019–2020 COG Poetry Award and a finalist for the 2021 Mississippi Review Prize in poetry. She is an assistant professor at DigiPen Institute of Technology, where she teaches creative writing and literature.

Teresa Leo is the author of two books of poetry, *Bloom in Reverse* (University of Pittsburgh Press) and *The Halo Rule*, winner of the Elixir Press Editors' Prize. She is the recipient of a Pew fellowship, a Leeway Foundation grant, two Pennsylvania Council on the Arts fellowships, and the Richard Peterson Poetry Prize from *Crab Orchard Review*. She works at the University of Pennsylvania.

Denise Leto is a queer multidisciplinary poet, writer, and dance dramaturge with a neuro-speech disability. Her current project, *home (Body)* is a collaborative dance/poetry/video installation and performance at the Santa Cruz Museum of Art and History. She cocreated the *San Francisco Baylands Eco-Poetry Project*. Her work has appeared in numerous publications, recently in *Orion, Baest, About Place: Practices of Hope, Rogue Agent, Mollyhouse, Hello/*

Goodbye Apocalypse and the *Italian American Review*. Poems are forthcoming in *Jacket2* and *Quarterly West*. She is the author of the poetry book for the dance/text art/performance exploring embodied and vocal difference, *Your Body is Not a Shark*. She does cross-genre, disability culture work with Olimpias Art Collective. She recently completed her poetry manuscript *The Body is a Wild Summons*.

Raymond Luczak is the author and editor of thirty books, including *once upon a twin: poems* (Gallaudet University Press), *Compassion, Michigan: The Ironwood Stories* (Modern History Press), and *QDA: A Queer Disability Anthology* (Squares & Rebels). His work has appeared in *Poetry, Prairie Schooner*, and elsewhere. He is an inaugural Zoeglossia Fellow.

Jennifer Maritza McCauley is a writer, editor, and professor. She received a National Endowment for the Arts fellowship in prose, and awards from Best of the Net, Independent Publisher Book Awards, and Academy of American Poets. She also received a Pushcart Prize Special Mention. She is presently a fiction editor at *Pleiades*. She is the author of *SCAR ON/SCAR OFF* (Stalking Horse Press 2017), a cross-genre collection, and *When Trying to Return Home* (Counterpoint 2023), a short story collection. She is an assistant professor in literature and creative writing at the University of Houston–Clear Lake.

Kyle McCord is the author of five books of poetry including National Poetry Series Finalist *Magpies in the Valley of Oleanders* (Trio House Press 2016). He has work featured or forthcoming in *AGNI, Blackbird, Boston Review, The Gettysburg Review, The Harvard Review, The Kenyon Review, Ploughshares, Tri-Quarterly,* and elsewhere. McCord received grants or awards from the Academy of American Poets, the Vermont Studio Center, and the Baltic Writing Residency. Currently he serves as Executive Editor of Gold Wake Press. He teaches in Des Moines, Iowa.

Rusty Morrison has been the cofounder and copublisher of *Omnidawn* since 2001. Her latest book, *Risk*, will be published by Black Ocean in Spring 2024. Her other five books include *After Urgency* (Tupelo's Dorset Prize), *the true keeps calm biding its story* (Ahsahta's Sawtooth Prize, James Laughlin Award, N. California Book Award, and DiCastagnola Award from PSA), and, most recently, *Beyond the Chainlink* (Ahsahta; finalist for the NCIB Award and NCB Award). She was awarded a fellowship by UC Berkeley Art Research Center's Poetry and the Senses Program (in the program's inaugural year of 2020). Her poems have appeared on the Poetry Foundation website, on their podcast series *Poetry Now*, in *Colorado Review, Fence, Iowa Review, Poetry Daily,* and elsewhere. She has taught in MFA programs, been a visiting poet at colleges, and teaches workshops through *Omnidawn* and elsewhere. For more info, see her website: rustymorrison.com.

Naomi Ortiz is a poet, writer, facilitator, and visual artist whose intersectional work focuses on self-care for activists, disability justice, climate action, and relationship with place. Ortiz is the author of *Sustaining Spirit: Self-Care for Social Justice* (Reclamation Press). They are a 2021–2022 Border Narrative Grant Awardee for their multidisciplinary project, *Complicating Conversations.* Their nonfiction contributions can be found in numerous publications, including *Poetry, Geez Magazine, Rooted in Rights, Feminist Wire,* and found in anthologies such as *Resistance and Hope: Essays by Disabled People.* Their visual art has been shown through a variety of venues, including in the Syracuse Cultural Workers Peace Calendar. As a Disabled Mestiza living in the Arizona US-Mexico borderlands, they are passionate about organizing with the Southern Arizona Community Care Collective (Colectivo de Beinestar Comunitario). For more info, see their website: NaomiOrtiz.com.

Carl Phillips is the author of sixteen books of poetry, most recently *Then the War: And Selected Poems 2007–2020* (Farrar, Straus & Giroux 2022). His honors include the 2021 Jackson Prize, the Aiken Taylor Award for Modern American Poetry, the Kingsley Tufts Award, a Lambda Literary Award, the PEN/USA Award for Poetry, and fellowships from the Guggenheim Foundation, the Library of Congress, the American Academy of Arts and Letters, and the Academy of American Poets. Phillips has also written three prose books, most recently *My Trade Is Mystery: Seven Meditations from a Life in Writing* (Yale University Press 2022); and he has translated the *Philoctetes of Sophocles* (Oxford University Press 2004). He teaches at Washington University in St. Louis.

Kevin Prufer's most recent book, *The Fears,* was published by Copper Canyon Press in 2023. He is the author of, among others, *How He Loved Them* (Four Way Books 2018), *Churches* (2014), *In a Beautiful Country* (2011), and *National Anthem* (2008). He's also coeditor of *New European Poets* (Graywolf Press 2008), *Literary Publishing in the 21st Century* (Milkweed Editions 2016), and *Into English: Poems, Translations, Commentaries* (Graywolf Press 2017). Among Prufer's awards and honors are four Pushcart prizes and multiple *Best American Poetry* selections, numerous awards from the Poetry Society of America, the Prairie Schooner/Strousse Award, and fellowships from the National Endowment for the Arts and the Lannan Foundation.

TC Tolbert identifies as a trans and genderqueer feminist, collaborator, mover, and poet. S/he is author of *Gephyromania* (Ahsahta Press 2014 and rereleased in 2022 by Nightboat Books) and five chapbooks and coeditor of *Troubling the Line: Trans and Genderqueer Poetry and Poetics* (Nightboat Books 2013). TC was awarded an Academy of American Poets' Laureate Fellowship in 2019 for his work with trans, nonbinary, and queer folks as Tucson's Poet Laureate. S/he also loves collaborating with wood. For more, see tctolbert.com.

Tanaya Winder is an author, singer-songwriter, and motivational speaker who comes from an intertribal lineage of Southern Ute, Pyramid Lake Paiute, and Duckwater Shoshone Nations, where she is an enrolled citizen. She is a 2016 National Center for American Indian Enterprise Development "40 Under 40" emerging American Indian leader. Winder cofounded *As/Us: A Space for Women of the World,* a literary magazine publishing works by BIPOC women. Winder's poetry collections include *Words Like Love* and *Why Storms are Named After People and Bullets Remain Nameless.* Her specialties include youth and women empowerment, healing trauma through art, creative writing workshops, and mental wellness advocacy. Winder's performances and talks blend storytelling, singing, and spoken word to teach about different expressions of love and "heartwork."

Jane Wong is the author of *How to Not Be Afraid of Everything* from Alice James Books (2021) and *Overpour from Action Books* (2016). Her debut memoir, *Meet Me Tonight in Atlantic City,* is forthcoming from Tin House in 2023. She is an associate professor of creative writing at Western Washington University. Her poems can be found in places such as *Best American Nonrequired Reading 2019, POETRY, AGNI, The Kenyon Review,* and others. Her essays have appeared in places such as *McSweeney's, Black Warrior Review,* and *This is the Place: Women Writing About Home.* A Kundiman fellow, she is the recipient of fellowships and residencies from the US Fulbright Program, Harvard's Woodberry Poetry Room, Bread Loaf, Hedgebrook, and others.